The
Road
to Calm

WORKBOOK

The Road to Calm

WORKBOOK

Life-Changing Tools
to Stop Runaway Emotions

CAROLYN DAITCH

AND

LISSAH LORBERBAUM

W.W. NORTON & COMPANY

Independent Publishers Since 1923

New York / London

Interior illustrations by Diana Elisabeth Dube, ded7881@gmail.com

For information about permission to reproduce selections from this book,
write to Permissions, W. W. Norton & Company, Inc.,
500 Fifth Avenue, New York, NY 10110

For information about special discounts for bulk purchases, please contact
W. W. Norton Special Sales at specialsales@wwnorton.com or 800-233-4830

Manufacturing by Edwards Brothers Malloy
Book design by Carole Desnoes
Production manager: Christine Critelli

Library of Congress Cataloging-in-Publication Data

Names: Daitch,
Carolyn, author. | Lorberbaum, Lissah, author.
Title: The road to calm
workbook : life changing tools to stop runaway emotions / Carolyn
Daitch, Lissah Lorberbaum.
Description: First edition. | New York : W.W. Norton & Company, 2016. |
    Includes bibliographical references and
index.
Identifiers: LCCN 2015035640 | ISBN 9780393708417 (pbk.)
Subjects:
LCSH: Anxiety—Treatment. | Stress management.
Classification: LCC RC531
.D354 2016 | DDC 616.85/2206—dc23
LC record available at
http://lccn.loc.gov/2015035640

W. W. Norton & Company, Inc.
500 Fifth Avenue, New York, N.Y. 10110
www.wwnorton.com

W. W. Norton & Company Ltd.
Castle House, 75/76 Wells Street, London W1T 3QT

1 2 3 4 5 6 7 8 9 0

This book is dedicated to our clients,
whose courage and commitment to their growth
continue to inspire us.

Between stimulus and response there is a space.
In that space is our power to choose our response.
In our response lies our growth and our freedom.

—VIKTOR FRANKL

Contents

Acknowledgments

If not for the many clinicians who applied the tools from *The Affect Regulation Toolbox* with their clients and enthusiastically shared their successes, this workbook would never have come to fruition. So first and foremost, we would like to acknowledge our colleagues.

We would also like to express deep gratitude to Deborah Malmud at W.W. Norton for consistently encouraging the project, coaxing along its progress with enthusiasm, and bringing keen insight to the editorial process. We are indeed fortunate to have her at the helm of our book. Cindy Barrilleaux, writing coach and editor, brought patience, much-needed laughter, and brilliant editorial skills. We are better writers as a result of her influence. She is truly a gift and we cherish her friendship.

We also thank the team at W.W. Norton for their support, professionalism, and expertise. Thanks to Alison Lewis, Elizabeth Baird, Angela Riley, Jessie Hughes, and Nathan Cohan. Thanks as well to Leslie Anglin for her careful copyediting. We are especially indebted to the skillful, diligent work of audio engineers Denis Pilon and Ted Jacobs. The audio component of this workbook would not be what it is without their tireless efforts. Special thanks also go to Helen Franklin for being such a good reader and friend. Also to Laurie Epstein Kach and Susan Barnett for reading early drafts of the manuscript. And finally immense gratitude goes to friend and husband Russ Graham for his unfailing support and patience.

Introduction from Carolyn Daitch

In 2007, I wrote the *Affect Regulation Toolbox*, which drew from my 25 years of experience as a psychologist helping clients live their lives with less emotional suffering. Although it was written for mental health professionals, therapists often recommended it to their clients.

The response to the book was overwhelmingly positive, and for years therapists and clients have asked me to write a version of the book geared toward people, whether in therapy or not, in need of quick and easy-to-implement tools to stop runaway emotions. When W.W. Norton invited me to write a workbook based on the *Affect Regulation Toolbox*, I had the perfect opportunity to respond to these requests. I enlisted psychotherapist Lissah Lorberbaum as my coauthor, and together we created *The Road to Calm Workbook: Life-Changing Tools to Stop Runaway Emotions*.

While the *Affect Regulation Toolbox* was written for clinicians, *The Road to Calm Workbook* is written for a lay audience. Further, this workbook offers tools for a broader range of emotional challenges than I covered in the *Toolbox*. In addition to providing help with anxiety and interpersonal triggers, this book addresses other common precursors of emotional flooding, including abandonment, hopelessness, explosive anger, feelings of being judged or shamed, and betrayal. This broader scope widens the impact and applicability of *The Road to Calm Workbook*.

About the Book

The Road to Calm Workbook offers a practical mix of teaching and exercises. You will learn how and why healthy emotions can become overwhelming and potentially destructive. The book describes the psychophysiological arousal that happens in the nervous system when a person is flooded by emotions. Gaining this understanding is the first step in regaining control of runaway emotions.

The workbook then introduces the STOP Solution for calming emotional flooding. This approach has proved effective in decades of experience with clients. The STOP Solution provides a methodical protocol of easy-to-use tools that can be applied when readers experience difficult-to-manage emotions. The tools have specific and individualized applicability to the most commonly experienced triggers. To reinforce the effectiveness of each tool, the workbook includes guided imagery exercises, opportunities to create positive self-statements, and space for personal reflections after practicing each tool. In addition, the workbook points readers to corresponding audio recordings and a downloadable companion app to facilitate their practice of the exercises as they go through the workbook. The tools and their accompanying written exercises, audio exercises, and companion app provide a gentle and reliable program that leads to calm, resilience, and well-being.

How It Is Organized

The Road to Calm Workbook is divided into two parts. Part I, Understanding Emotional Flooding, lays the foundation for understanding why and when emotional flooding occurs. Stories and vivid examples of situations that trigger emotional overwhelm expand the readers' grasp of how others experience intense emotions. This part makes readers aware of the unhealthy extremes of three basic emotions: fear, anger, and sadness. Readers also learn about the three parts of the brain and how they relate to emotional flooding. Part I explores the importance of attuned emotional connection in relationships and how emotional flooding can disrupt that connection.

In addition, Part I includes a wide variety of graphs, flow charts, self-assessment tools, and opportunities for self-reflection and journaling to help readers apply the material and tools so they can gain mastery of their runaway emotions.

Part II, The Road to Self-Regulation, introduces and teaches the Daily Stress Inoculation, a daily practice for relaxing and lowering your baseline levels of emotional reactivity. This practice increases the reader's sense of calm throughout the day and decreases the likelihood of emotional flooding. Clear instructions for the Daily Stress Inoculation are followed by tips about how to make this practice a daily habit, an automated reminder that readers can set using the workbook's companion app, and a log for tracking practice.

After teaching the Daily Stress Inoculation protocol, Part II teaches the STOP Solution and the 12 tools for emotional self-regulation. STOP refers to a clear, concrete sequence of actions: Scan thoughts, feelings, and sensations; Take a time-out; Overcome initial flooding; and Put the tools into practice. Among the tools readers will learn are Mindfulness with Detached Observation, Remembering Successes, the Wise Self, Positive Future-Focusing, and Dialing Down Reactivity. Practice of each of these tools is essential so that whenever readers sense the onset of an emotional overreaction, they can apply the appropriate tools. The STOP Solution can stop emotional overwhelm, leading to the equilibrium needed to experience emotions with less reactivity and greater stability. The result is freedom from the emotional patterns that create suffering and damage relationships.

The workbook is accompanied by an audio program designed to guide readers through the use of each tool and The Road to Calm Companion App to enhance the tools' use. The workbook teaches readers how to apply particular tools for specific states of inner turmoil, such as panic, hopelessness, frustration, and worry. Readers also learn how to apply the tools to an array of interpersonal triggers, including betrayal, feeling judged or shamed, fear of abandonment, and feeling misunderstood.

A noteworthy feature of this book is that it prescribes sequences of tools for each of the emotional triggers that lead to affect dysregulation. The strength of this approach to emotional reactivity lies not in a quick fix by one modality but in the combination and range of all the tools, interventions, exercises, journaling, and guided reflections. These together provide an array of individualized solutions to the pervasive problem of emotional overwhelm.

How to Use the Workbook

Because the book addresses specific emotional problems and situations, it may be tempting for the reader to skip directly to the instructions for the emotional challenge that is presently troubling him or her. However, in doing so, the reader will overlook the essential foundation of learning the information about emotions and emotional flooding and its neurological basis.

Instead, we advise readers to go through this workbook in the order it is presented and to do all the exercises and written reflections. As readers become comfortable with each exercise, they will discover the benefits of regular practice. Experience shows that consistent application of the tools results in profound changes in reactive styles.

To better implement the tools, we also recommend that readers transfer the audio tracks that accompany this workbook onto a portable audio player (such as an mp3 player or smartphone) and download the workbook's free companion app to a smartphone. The Road to Calm Companion App can be downloaded to Android or iPhone devices from the Google Play or Apple App Store. Once the free app is downloaded, readers can also upgrade to the premium version of the companion app, which offers a variety of additional features.

It is our hope, similar to the goal of the *Affect Regulation Toolbox*, to provide you with an arsenal of tools that will help you move out of the reactivity rut and into a calm and more resilient response to the inevitable stressors of life.

PART I

Understanding Emotional Flooding

1 Understanding Emotional Flooding

. . . feelings can't be ignored, no matter how unjust or ungrateful they seem.

—ANNE FRANK

EVERYONE HAS HAD THE EXPERIENCE OF BEING OVERWHELMED, OR FLOODED, with emotion. It's part of being human. Unfortunately, these strong surges of emotion, which we'll refer to in this workbook as *emotional flooding*, can take a toll on your day-to-day functioning, your work, and the relationships with people in your life. If you've picked up this workbook, it's possible that you are experiencing some of the painful consequences of emotional flooding. It's nearly impossible to navigate inevitable life challenges, both big and small, if you can't manage your emotions well. Fear, anger, anxiety, and sadness, if unchecked and mismanaged, can drive your life in unfortunate directions.

Excessive emotionality can make it difficult to respond effectively to the inevitable ups and downs of any given day. Reactions, feelings, and thoughts—and the decisions that you make in response—become influenced more by anger, fear, or sadness than by reason. In this way, uncontainable emotion can hijack your best intentions. This can lead to the loss of jobs, friendships, and romantic relationships. It can also fragment relationships with family members. Both you and those around you can feel at the mercy of your emotions, constantly on guard for the tidal wave that might arise in this moment or the next.

To determine whether emotional flooding significantly impacts you, ask yourself the following:

- Does the intensity of my emotion ever interfere with my functioning or my relationships?
- Might an objective observer think that the degree of emotion I sometimes experience is excessive relative to the situation at hand?

If you answered "yes" to either or both of these questions, you most likely experience *emotional flooding*: strong surges of emotion that come on rapidly, persist with overpowering force, interfere with your functioning in the present, and resist being quelled by logic-based thoughts.

There are four crucial components of emotional flooding:

- the high intensity of the emotion (including an intense physiological response)
- the intensity of emotion is often out of proportion to the situation you are responding to
- an inability to dampen the emotional intensity
- the interference with your functioning in the present moment

This chapter will help you better understand emotional flooding and its impact on your life. This is the first step in learning to manage your emotional flooding.

Emotions in Everyday Life

Life constantly presents challenges:

- *Your boss gives you unfavorable feedback.*
- *Your friend calls last minute to cancel your lunch plans with her.*
- *Construction on the road makes you late to work.*
- *A driver absentmindedly drifts into your lane, forcing you to slam on the brakes to avoid an accident.*
- *You are distracted by a phone call and the dinner burns.*
- *You've just had to repeat the same simple request to your spouse for the umpteenth time.*
- *You know that your teenager hit "snooze" on the alarm clock for the third time, and the carpool is coming in 15 minutes.*

This is all part of the ebb and flow of daily life. And just as not all of life is negative, neither are all emotions negative. The ability to feel intense emotion is also a gift:

— *You are inspired by a piece of music.*
— *You fall passionately in love.*
— *You walk into your parents' home on Thanksgiving and smell the turkey in the oven and the fragrant smell of a pumpkin pie.*
— *You see a coworker, friend, or even stranger smile in response to something kind you have just done.*
— *You touch a baby's face and see her smile.*

There are days when you catch that gorgeous sunset. And then there are days when you're stuck at the office and miss it. There are moments when you (and possibly family members in various stages of protest) are rushing out of the house in the morning, and then there are the moments when you're sinking into your couch in the evening, feeling how nice it is to take off your shoes and put your feet up. In the continuous flow of time, all of these experiences are interspersed. And with these experiences, emotion—in all its many forms—is inevitable. Frustration, gratitude, anger, joy, comfort, discomfort, nervousness, calm—the experience of the vast array of emotional states is part of being human and alive.

Problems arise, however, when the intensity of emotion that you experience is disproportionate to the situation at hand. When this happens, you may get stuck in this intense emotion, unable to let the next emotion flow in. This is when emotional flooding occurs.

SARAH: ANGER

Consider Sarah, who began worrying that her angry verbal outbursts were creating a home environment that was harmful to her children and destructive to her marriage. Sarah was an engineer with a demanding job and a long commute. Sarah's husband Terry, a freelance writer, worked from home. He readily admitted that housekeeping was not high on his priority list. He would let dishes accumulate in the sink and piles of papers on the kitchen table throughout the day. Upon arriving home, the general state of the house, combined with her fatigue and hunger, would often put Sarah over the edge. She would slam her briefcase on the counter, bang the cupboards when she fixed dinner, and respond sharply to her children's requests. One evening, after a particularly bad tirade, Sarah called her sister for support. "I hate myself because I feel like I'm becoming just like mom, but I find myself yelling at Terry and the kids and berating them for being lazy and inconsiderate. I know it's reasonable for me to simply ask that everyone pick up after themselves. But I can't seem to do that without flying off the handle and yelling at everyone—even though I know that doesn't help, and only makes things worse. And I know Terry's not happy. How could he be? I'm not happy either."

NICOLE: LONELINESS

Nicole, a 34-year-old attorney, came into therapy expressing her hopelessness at finding and maintaining a committed relationship. "I'm so lonely I can't bear it. I just want to find someone to love who can love me back and not leave me," Nicole said as she wiped away a tear. "I'm so sorry, but it really is scary to think that I will never get married, never have children, and that I will die alone." When asked what she thought was interfering with her relationships, she sighed and said, "Oh, I already know what the problem is. Whenever I get involved with a guy, I start to worry that he will leave me, and even though I don't want to, even though I know better, I start getting clingy, possessive, and overreact when he doesn't call me or text me back right away. All of my courtroom composure goes straight out the window. I just can't seem to stop myself. And then I am no longer the competent successful woman whom they were attracted to but a sniveling, weak, overwhelming little girl. And who would want that? So they all leave me. Every one of them leaves me. I am so stuck, I can't stand it."

MARK: DEPRESSION

Mark had a long history of depressive episodes. Following his divorce, however, he plummeted into severe depression, feeling alone and as if his whole world had turned upside down. Lost in feelings of remorse, he ruminated about his inadequacies as a husband. Everything about him felt raw and he began to isolate from his friends and coworkers. What's more, Mark felt chronically tired and unmotivated. At work, his supervisor expressed concern about his lack of concentration and lowered productivity. Mark interpreted this feedback as further confirmation of his inadequacies, and his depression worsened.

Like Sarah, Nicole, and Mark, you may feel at the mercy of your emotions. Emotions, in and of themselves, are neither good nor bad. Even intense emotions have a time and place in which their expression is adaptive, as the following section discusses.

The Essentials of Emotions

The ability to experience strong surges of emotion, especially fear, anger, and sadness, can serve you in countless ways. Fear and anger help alert you to the possibility that some aspect of your well-being might be in jeopardy. Once the alert signal is sounded, the experience of fear or anger then helps your mind and body mobilize to determine if a threat is present and to protect you if it is. Unlike fear and anger, the experience of sadness doesn't set off alarm bells to mobilize you into protective action. However, sadness can help protect you by motivating you to see the value of and preserve what is important in your life. First let's define what these emotions are and take a look at the ways in which they facilitate our ability to survive and thrive in the world.

FEAR: a strong physical and psychological response to perceived danger typically accompanied by uneasy feelings; physical discomfort; worried, obsessive, or catastrophic thoughts; and rigid and avoidant behaviors.

ANGER: a physical and psychological response that mobilizes natural defense systems to respond to perceived threats to your or others' well-being.

SADNESS: a psychological response to loss or disappointment often accompanied by feelings of hopelessness, despondency, and sorrow or grief.

FEAR

The surge of fear you experience when you register that a pedestrian has stepped into the street directly in your car's path helps your body mobilize to slam on your brakes. Your fear of having an accident, motivated by your desire to protect yourself and the pedestrian from harm, helps you mobilize your resources to avoid a collision.

Fear is related to and often leads to a pervasive sense of anxiety. The fear you experience, for instance, when you anticipate an upcoming speech at work can lead to worry and anxiety. However, it might also motivate you to prepare well for your presentation. The anxiety generated by the possibility of giving a poor presentation prompts you to take action that will enhance your performance in a potentially stressful situation. When the day of the speech arrives, the anxiety can also help you remain alert and on your toes during the presentation itself. Whether you're saving a life or saving yourself from embarrassment, fear and anxiety are vital to maintaining your safety and security.

Can you describe an instance in which **FEAR** has served you well?

_____
_____
_____
_____

ANGER

Anger is an adaptive response intended to protect us. When mobilized as physical or verbal aggression, anger wards off physical or psychological harm by an external threat. It helps you fight off attacks.

The anger or frustration that you often experience in relationships, whether with friends, coworkers, or family members, also can be an indicator that some component of your psychological well-being is not being respected. For example, the anger felt in response to your partner's sharp criticism helps you recognize that your partner isn't responding to you with kindness. Your anger provides the impetus that drives you to action. You might then request that your partner communicate criticism more constructively.

Can you describe an instance in which **ANGER** has served you well?

_____
_____
_____
_____

SADNESS

Sadness is an inevitable experience in life. Sometimes it is transient, but at other times it can hold you like an unrelenting vise. It is often connected to loss. For well-being, everyone needs care, connection, compassion, love, and support. If you lose someone you care about, whether due to death, a breakup, or leaving for college, you may feel very sad. The sadness of loss can also be related to other circumstances, such as losing a job or not getting into graduate school.

In some cases, sadness can motivate you to choose more wisely to prevent future loss. In instances in which you cannot regain a loss, sadness, in the form of grief, helps you to fully acknowledge the gift of the relationships or experiences you have lost.

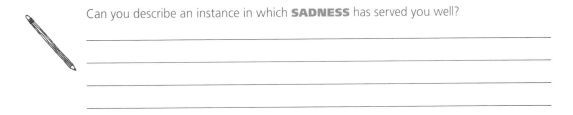

Can you describe an instance in which **SADNESS** has served you well?

_____

_____

_____

_____

The ability to experience a range of emotions is crucial to human beings' ability to thrive in life. However, problems can arise when the level of anger, fear, sadness, or any other challenging emotion becomes overwhelming and keeps you from functioning effectively.

Emotional Flooding

There are many times in life where strong emotions are appropriate. However, the same intense fear, anxiety, or anger that can save your life can be maladaptive if applied in the wrong context. Rather than viewing these emotions as either good or bad, it is more helpful to ask yourself if the intensity of your emotions interferes with your functioning in the present moment. If your anxiety, fear, anger, or sadness is too high, it no longer helps you respond optimally to your situation or environment and often becomes a hindrance rather than an aid.

For example, if knowledge of an upcoming public speaking engagement causes you to become so worried that you either don't prepare for the presentation or you freeze the moment you start to present, anxiety has become a hindrance rather than an aid. Or if you experienced the same surge of fear that helped you avoid hitting the pedestrian *every* time you attempted to drive, driving would become highly stressful. You might even find yourself avoiding driving altogether, leading to a dependency on others to drive you everywhere. Likewise, if you responded to your partner's criticism with the intensity of anger you would need to defend against a physical threat, you would escalate the conflict and be hurtful to your partner as well. If you still felt the *same* degree of sadness a year after a relationship broke up that you did after the first week, you might be stuck in grief and hopelessness. Rather than learning from your past mistakes and moving forward into new relationships, your sadness could lead to hours of ruminating on mistakes you made in a relationship that is long gone.

In all these instances, emotional flooding takes a huge toll.

EMOTIONAL FLOODING: A QUICK CHECKUP

In the last week, how often have the following feelings created suffering for you?

Feeling	Never	Rarely	Sometimes	Frequently	Almost Always
worried	1	2	3	4	5
panicked	1	2	3	4	5
intolerance of physical discomfort or distress	1	2	3	4	5
hopeless	1	2	3	4	5
frustrated	1	2	3	4	5
explosive anger	1	2	3	4	5
abandoned	1	2	3	4	5
betrayed	1	2	3	4	5
controlled	1	2	3	4	5
criticized	1	2	3	4	5
judged	1	2	3	4	5
shamed	1	2	3	4	5
misunderstood	1	2	3	4	5

lack of empathy from another	1	2	3	4	5
resentment	1	2	3	4	5
defeated/hopeless	1	2	3	4	5

Take note of any times that you circled a 4 or 5. In later chapters of this book you will have the opportunity to learn tools to ease this type of emotional flooding when it arises.

UNDERSTANDING EMOTIONAL FLOODING

The metaphor "emotional flooding" captures the nature of the psychophysiological state it describes: floods arise quickly, strike with overpowering force, are overwhelming to experience, and leave destruction in their wake. Often people feel ashamed and frustrated by their inability to dampen the intensity of emotion that arises during these floods. This is why it's important to understand the biologically based reasons that it's so hard to quell emotional flooding. This requires an understanding of how your brain works. In his groundbreaking book *The Emotional Brain*, neuroscientist Joseph LeDoux (1996) writes that the brain is wired in such a way that it is far easier to become flooded with emotion than to self-regulate and manage the emotion with reason. This struggle is not only understandable—it's instinctual.

It is helpful to grasp some key neuropsychological processes at play when you experience strong emotion. This begins with an understanding of the *three-part brain*.

THE THREE-PART BRAIN

Your brain is composed of many different structures. Like the organs in the rest of your body, each structure performs an array of functions and works together with the other structures in the brain to ensure optimal functioning. Based on their location and the tasks each structure performs, neuroscientists have grouped the brain structures into three different "families," or parts. Although the three parts that make up your triune or three-part brain are known by a few different names, in this workbook we will refer to them as the "hindbrain," the "midbrain," and the "forebrain." Because the brain's functioning is highly complex, it's important to emphasize that the three-part brain is a conceptual

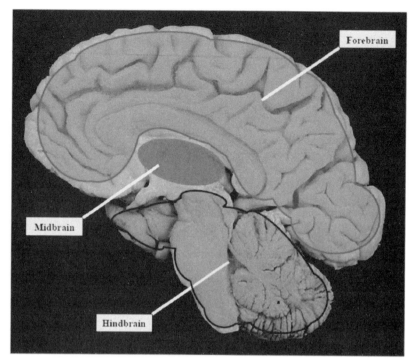

Figure 1.1 The Three-Part Brain. Used with permission: New Harbinger Publications, Inc. Copyright © 2012 by Carolyn Daitch and Lissah Lorberbaum. (This diagram presents a visual approximation of the hindbrain, midbrain, and forebrain based on MacLean's triune brain theory. However, the individual brain structures within these three regions are not neatly encapsulated within the areas this diagram depicts.)

simplification. There are many different ways to conceptualize the brain's functioning. With that in mind, learning how these three parts of your brain have historically been understood to function based on MacLean's triune brain theory is invaluable to your understanding of emotional flooding.

As is shown in Figure 1.1, the hindbrain is located toward the base of the brain near where the brain connects with your spinal column. The structures within the hindbrain perform tasks associated with the control of bodily functions basic to survival such as heart rate, breathing, and hunger. The midbrain, as we are representing it here, is located approximately in the middle of your brain and performs tasks associated with the experience of emotions, among other things.

The forebrain is located above the hindbrain and midbrain and is largely responsible for your ability to think logically and rationally. The forebrain is the most recent part of the brain in evolutionary development. The structures in the large forebrain enable humans to engage in complex thought and to communicate with written and spoken language.

The forebrain also acts as your voice of reason, allowing you to keep your impulses in check and evaluate the safety of your environment. It's responsible for that wise inner voice that reminds you not to spend your entire paycheck on that new entertainment system at the electronics store. It's also responsible for the calming voice that reassures you that there's no need for alarm, because the thump in the night that woke you was just the central heating kicking in and you're safe to go back to sleep.

When all three parts of the brain are operating ideally, they work together, providing *and responding to* each other's feedback. For example, when a loud bang startles you, the midbrain and hindbrain work together so you are instantly alert. Your heart begins pounding, your breathing quickens, and your entire body mobilizes in case action is needed. Meanwhile your forebrain comes online, scans the environment, and helps you use logic to interpret the sights, sensations, smells, or in this case, sounds of a possible threat. In this scenario the forebrain helps you discern that the sound was made by the central heating system. It relays to the other two parts of the brain that there's no need to sustain the call to arms, and the midbrain listens and powers down the fear response. Your heartbeat slows down. Thanks to the successful interplay of all three parts of your brain, your body prepares to ease back into sleep for the remainder of the night so you can get the rest you need—until that pesky alarm clock signals the start of your day.

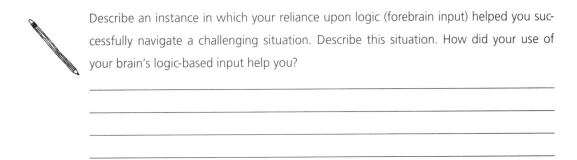

Describe an instance in which your reliance upon logic (forebrain input) helped you successfully navigate a challenging situation. Describe this situation. How did your use of your brain's logic-based input help you?

_____

_____

_____

_____

EMOTIONAL FLOODING AND THE
MIDBRAIN-FOREBRAIN DISCONNECT

But not all of us can power down so easily after our system gets revved. This marks the difference between becoming activated and getting flooded. When you are flooded with emotion, your midbrain becomes highly activated. When this

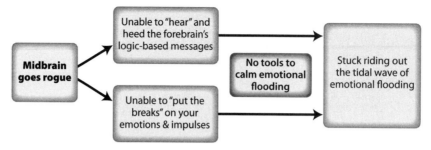

Figure 1.2 Key Components of Emotional Flooding

occurs, communication between your midbrain and your forebrain is interrupted and the midbrain takes center stage. No longer working together, the midbrain does not "hear" the input of the forebrain—the part of your brain that acts as the voice of reason, stepping in with logical appraisals of the situation to help you see that a heightened emotional response is not necessary. The forebrain aids in impulse control. When the forebrain and midbrain communicate optimally, the forebrain's messages to the midbrain help you keep your impulses in check. However, when it is unable to be calmed by reason or hear and heed the forebrain's messages, the midbrain steals the show, leaving you at the mercy of your emotions and your impulses. In effect, your midbrain has gone rogue. (See Figure 1.2.)

COMPARING THE INFLUENCE OF LOGIC VS. EMOTIONS

Think of the last time that you were emotionally flooded. Use Figure 1.3 to rate the comparative strengths of logic and emotion during that instance. On the chart, mark and shade in the relative strengths of each. You don't need to be concerned about being precise, just give your best "guestimate."

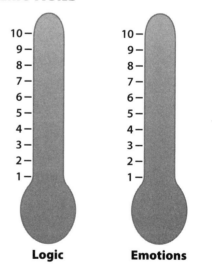

Figure 1.3

During the experience of emotional flooding, the rational words of the forebrain simply aren't sufficient to quell the flood of hyperactivation of the midbrain. Even the knowledge that the sound that startled you awake was the central heating won't stop your heart from racing, and you can *forget* about getting back to sleep any time soon. Or maybe the voice of logic tells you not to snap at your coworker because you can't afford a possible write-up. But that voice has little power over the anger brewing after his sarcastic retort. Imagine going to the beach and trying to stop a wave. Trying to stop overwhelming waves of emotion with reason alone is equally futile.

GAUGING THE STYLE AND IMPACT OF YOUR EMOTIONAL FLOODING

A preliminary step in regaining the ability to intervene in your own emotional flooding involves clearly identifying the ways emotional flooding manifests in your life. The following questionnaire allows you to get a sense of how frequently you experience emotional flooding and its effect on your relationships. It's important to refrain from self-judgment as you consider these questions. Just let your answers reflect how you honestly feel the majority of the time. Circle the answer that feels most true for you.

SELF-ASSESSMENT

1. I feel tense or on edge.	(1) Rarely or never (2) Sometimes	(3) Often (4) Very often
2. I have difficulty calming myself when I'm upset.	(1) Rarely or never (2) Sometimes	(3) Often (4) Very often
3. I have an easygoing temperament.	(4) Rarely or never (3) Sometimes	(2) Often (1) Very often
4. I feel intense waves of fear, anxiety, irritability, or sadness.	(1) Rarely or never (2) Sometimes	(3) Often (4) Very often
5. In the mornings, I wake up feeling agitated.	(1) Rarely or never (2) Sometimes	(3) Often (4) Very often
6. It's easy for me to fall asleep and stay asleep throughout the night.	(4) Rarely or never (3) Sometimes	(2) Often (1) Very often

7. I make a point of avoiding situations or places that cause me anxiety or worry.

(1) Rarely or never   (3) Often
(2) Sometimes   (4) Very often

8. I experience sudden, overwhelming, and unexpected waves of panic that seem to arise out of nowhere.

(1) Rarely or never   (3) Often
(2) Sometimes   (4) Very often

9. I worry about the future and what might go wrong.

(1) Rarely or never   (3) Often
(2) Sometimes   (4) Very often

10. I wish I were more at ease.

(1) Rarely or never   (3) Often
(2) Sometimes   (4) Very often

11. I experience uncomfortable physical sensations, such as stomach distress, headaches, or muscle tension or pain.

(1) Rarely or never   (3) Often
(2) Sometimes   (4) Very often

12. Decision making is stressful for me.

(1) Rarely or never   (3) Often
(2) Sometimes   (4) Very often

13. I experience crying spells.

(1) Rarely or never   (3) Often
(2) Sometimes   (4) Very often

14. I give up quickly because I don't think my efforts will make a difference.

(1) Rarely or never   (3) Often
(2) Sometimes   (4) Very often

15. I feel hopeless.

(1) Rarely or never   (3) Often
(2) Sometimes   (4) Very often

16. I am annoyed by other people.

(1) Rarely or never   (3) Often
(2) Sometimes   (4) Very often

17. I am disappointed by other people.

(1) Rarely or never   (3) Often
(2) Sometimes   (4) Very often

18. I am overwhelmed by stressful situations.

(1) Rarely or never   (3) Often
(2) Sometimes   (4) Very often

19. I experience strong cravings for food or substances which I find difficult to manage.

(1) Rarely or never   (3) Often
(2) Sometimes   (4) Very often

20. I am impulsive.

(1) Rarely or never   (3) Often
(2) Sometimes   (4) Very often

21. I am well disciplined.	(4) Rarely or never	(2) Often
	(3) Sometimes	(1) Very often
22. The intensity of my anger startles or frightens others.	(1) Rarely or never	(3) Often
	(2) Sometimes	(4) Very often
23. I feel irritable.	(1) Rarely or never	(3) Often
	(2) Sometimes	(4) Very often
24. I behave in ways that I regret.	(1) Rarely or never	(3) Often
	(2) Sometimes	(4) Very often
25. Friends and family experience my emotions as intense.	(1) Rarely or never	(3) Often
	(2) Sometimes	(4) Very often
26. I wish I had better self-control.	(1) Rarely or never	(3) Often
	(2) Sometimes	(4) Very often
27. I feel ashamed or guilty after exhibiting uncontrolled behavior or words.	(1) Rarely or never	(3) Often
	(2) Sometimes	(4) Very often
28. The people around me are negatively impacted by my lack of emotional containment.	(1) Rarely or never	(3) Often
	(2) Sometimes	(4) Very often

SCORING

If you circled a 3 or 4 on five or more questions, it is highly likely that emotional flooding is significantly impacting your life.

If you circled mostly 1's and 2's, emotional flooding has impacted you but does not frequently impinge on your daily functioning.

Regardless of the frequency of your emotional flooding, the ability to recognize your levels of arousal and to self-regulate accordingly is an asset in both your personal and professional life. The tools presented help create and sustain a daily relaxation regimen, and they can also significantly enhance your ability to engage in the present moment with a sense of calm and ease. As you progress through this workbook and apply the tools in your daily life, you can look forward to gaining enhanced self-regulation skills and increasing the stability in your relationships.

JOURNALING EXERCISE: THE TOLL OF EMOTIONAL FLOODING ————————

Journaling offers you the opportunity to synthesize and clarify your learning and thinking. It also helps you manage stress, explore your experience, and put things in perspective. The following questions offer you the opportunity to journal about your experience of emotional flooding. If you require more space than the lines provided, we encourage you to continue writing on additional sheets of paper.

How has your emotional flooding created suffering and struggle in your life?

_____

_____

_____

_____

_____

_____

_____

_____

_____

How has your emotional flooding impacted your personal relationships?

_____

_____

_____

_____

_____

_____

_____

_____

_____

How do you feel now that you have a better understanding of your own emotional flooding?

_____

_____

_____

_____

_____

_____

_____

Understanding the neurobiological underpinnings of emotional flooding provides a biological explanation of why reason alone cannot calm overwhelming emotions. The key to regulating emotional tidal waves is not talk or logic. To overcome emotional flooding, you need a powerful way to quiet the hyperactivation of the midbrain, enabling all three parts of the brain to return to their optimal state of equilibrium in which they can communicate with one another again. By learning and applying the tools in this workbook, you will be training your mind and body to effectively "speak" to the hyperactive midbrain. With this method, you can learn to manage your emotions, rather than having them control you (see Figure 1.4).

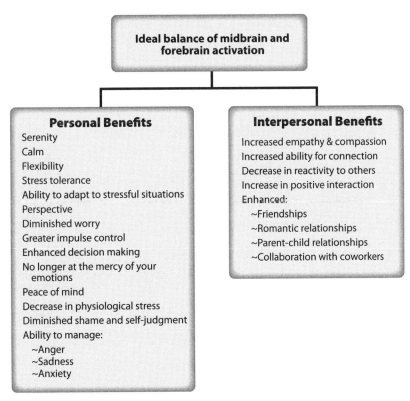

Figure 1.4 Ideal Balance of Midbrain and Forebrain Activation

Take-Away Points

- *Emotional flooding*: strong surges of emotion that come on rapidly, persist with overpowering force, and aren't easily quelled by logic.
- Emotional flooding doesn't exist in a vacuum. It not only affects you but also impacts your relationships.
- There are four characteristics of emotional flooding:
  - high intensity of the emotion (including an intense physiological response)
  - intensity of emotion is often out of proportion to the situation you are responding to
  - an inability to dampen the emotional intensity
  - the interference with your functioning in the present moment
- Key questions to ask yourself:
  - Does the intensity of my emotion ever interfere with my functioning or my relationships?
  - Might an objective observer think that the degree of emotion I sometimes experience is excessive relative to the situation at hand?
- The brain can be conceptualized as being divided into three parts:
  - The hindbrain (basic functions such as heart rate, breathing, etc.)
  - The midbrain (emotions)
  - The forebrain (logic, language, abstract thinking, and complex reasoning)
- When you experience emotional flooding, the midbrain goes rogue. When this happens, emotion roars and logic-based input from the forebrain comes across with the power of a whisper.

How Emotional Flooding Hurts

Man is not worried by real problems so much as by his imagined anxieties about real problems.

—EPICTETUS

BEFORE LEARNING TO APPLY THE 12 TOOLS FOR SPECIFIC EMOTIONAL FLOOD-ing, it is important to understand some of the ways that emotions manifest in your life. This chapter will help you identify some of the specific ways that various combinations of emotion can present challenges. For some, emotional flooding is a component of a psychological disorder. Others suffer greatly from runaway emotions even in the absence of any particular "disorder." Having a framework to better understand how intense emotions manifest will prepare you to implement the tools more effectively.

The Everyday Flow of Emotion

Consciousness is an emotion-filled experience. Every moment that you are awake (and even some of the moments you are asleep) you experience an unending tide of emotion. As you move through an average day, the major-ity of emotions you experience are not particularly remarkable (unless you are struggling with a particular psychological disorder or undergoing a huge life change or stressor). In fact, you often fail to register emotion at all. But you are constantly experiencing an ever-changing flow of emotion nevertheless (see Figure 2.1).

As emotions increase in intensity, you become more conscious of them. For instance, you might have enjoyed satisfaction, contentment, and pride

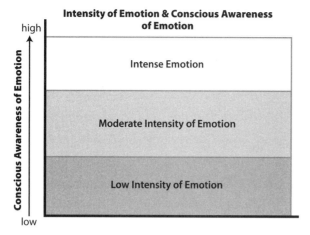

Figure 2.1

that came from a good performance review at work. You may have noticed relief and excitement as you headed home from work to enjoy the weekend. You often register a variety of levels of anger and aggravation when another driver snags a parking spot you had been patiently waiting for. You experience a wide range of sadness in response to loss, both big and small. Everyone has experienced and will experience all of the emotional challenges that this chapter and the next will address:

— Worry

— Panic

— Intolerance of physical discomfort or distress

— Loneliness

— Pervasive hopelessness

— Frustration

— Explosive anger

The goal of this workbook is not to teach you how to *never* feel the difficult emotions we identify. Rather, it is to teach you how to *modulate* the intensity of the emotion that you experience. Feeling an emotion is not the problem. Your ability to experience a vast range of emotions, and varying intensities of emotion, greatly enriches and enhances life. Emotional *flooding* becomes a problem, however, when you lack tools to check the intensity of a given emotion and suffer as a result.

Anxiety-, Depression-, and Anger-Related Disorders

"Anxiety's like a rocking chair. It gives you something to do,
but it doesn't get you very far."
                                                    —JODI PICOULT, novelist

Emotional flooding plays a key role in all psychological disorders. The tools this workbook teaches can lessen the emotional distress present with any psychological disorder you may be experiencing. The disorders outlined here relate generally to anxiety, depression, and anger. However, if you have another psychological disorder (other common ones include eating disorders and addictions), the tools in this workbook can help you when emotional flooding arises.

If you relate to any disorders discussed in this chapter, the good news is that there are many avenues for change, healing, and relief. In addition to using the tools in this workbook (for each disorder, specific tools are provided), there are many resources available to facilitate your healing journey. We encourage you to seek additional information on any particular disorder that is manifesting in your life. To assist this endeavor, we've included a list of additional resources in Appendix A. You can also consider seeking support in the form of professional counseling. However, identifying the nature of your particular challenges is the first step in this process.

GENERALIZED ANXIETY DISORDER

If you are a chronic worrier about what disaster is looming around each bend in the road (this is called *anticipatory anxiety*), you may be suffering from a common anxiety disorder called generalized anxiety disorder (GAD).

Angela, aged 41, was a self-described chronic worrier. Plagued by worry for about as long as she could remember, she finally decided to go to a therapist for help. Angela's description of her problem to her therapist captures the nature of GAD.

"I always prepare for the worst," Angela said. "My mother says that I borrow trouble and that I suffer in advance. I worry particularly about my children—their health, whether they are hanging with the right kids. I even worry about them getting into a good college, even though they are only in middle school. I have been told I'm overprotective and then I worry about that, afraid that I am hurting the boys. Sometimes it gets so bad, I get awful stomachaches. I can't even escape through sleep, because I can't turn off my mind at night, so I'm constantly tired. Then I worry if I'll ever feel rested again, or if I'll get into a car accident because I'm so exhausted . . . and then what if the boys are in the car."

GAD is experienced in three arenas: cognitive, emotional, and physical. The cognitive dimension shows up as worried thoughts you experience with an intensity that is probably out of proportion to the issue you are worried about. A host of "what ifs" plague your mind. You may worry excessively about your health, finances, and work issues, along with unrelenting worry about your children or other loved ones. You may find it hard to make decisions, worrying that you will make the wrong one and won't be able to accept the consequences.

In the emotional dimension, you may feel constantly on edge, jumpy, irritable, and wired. You may feel chronically vulnerable in a world that seems uncertain and unsafe, even though you are not aware of the thoughts behind your feelings. Furthermore, you may feel lonely and isolated in your despair, imagining that no one is suffering like you are and that others will not understand your emotions.

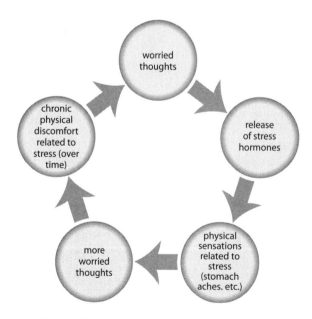

Figure 2.2 The Vicious Cycle of Generalized Anxiety Disorder

In the physical arena, you may experience stomach distress, headaches, and back or other muscular pain. The discomfort in your body results from excessive levels of stress hormones that circulate in your body for sustained periods of time. Most people with GAD not only experience discomfort in their bodies, they also worry about their physical symptoms. So you may suffer from an insidious cycle in which worried thoughts create the release of stress hormones, which fuels physical discomfort, which fuels even more worried thoughts, which then heightens the chronic physical complaints, ad infinitum. This vicious cycle can also lead to difficulties falling asleep or staying asleep throughout the night.

PANIC ATTACKS

Panic attacks are characterized by assaults of intense fear that often seem to come from nowhere with an intensity that feels unmanageable and unstoppable. If you experience a panic attack, you are beset by fear so intense that it feels overwhelming and you feel as if you are losing control. A hallmark of a panic attack is a strong physical reaction. It is not uncommon for people to think they are having a heart attack, because the panic attack often elicits cardiac sensations such as a racing heartbeat, shortness of breath, and hot or cold sweats. These symptoms occur because your nervous system has been flooded with stress hormones and moves into a fight-or-flight mode. But the misattribution that these physical symptoms indicate a life-threatening ailment serves to fuel the panic even more.

Concurrent with intense physical distress, you may also experience the strange sense that what you are experiencing doesn't feel real; you know you aren't dreaming, but somehow you're not experiencing "reality" the way you normally do. As a result, the world just doesn't feel quite right. You may feel as if you are observing yourself from the outside or detached from your normal sense of reality. This is called *depersonalization.* Or you may feel like your environment is unreal. This is called *derealization.* In any case, the inability to calm the feelings of impending doom can feed into a fear that you are going crazy. Of course, this is not the case. Nevertheless, panic attacks are jarring, acutely distressing experiences that leave most people hoping never to experience another one.

PANIC DISORDER

Many people who have had panic attacks do not necessarily go on to develop panic *disorder*. Panic disorder has two key components *in addition to* the experience of one or more panic attacks. As we mentioned earlier, if you've had a panic attack you will most likely have a very strong desire to never experience another panic attack again. For those who go on to develop panic disorder, this urgency to avoid another panic attack, combined with the fear that more panic attacks are inevitable, creates an insidious cycle.

There are three main components of panic disorder:

1. One or more panic attacks (which typically last less than 20 minutes but are experienced with great intensity)
2. Worry about when and where the next panic attack will occur
3. Avoidance of the places and situations where you have experienced panic or are afraid a panic attack is likely to occur

If you have panic disorder, you devote a good deal of mental energy trying to lessen the chance that you will suffer more panic attacks. Therefore, you seek to limit your exposure to any environment or situation that might be likely to trigger an attack. Among the common places people with panic disorder may avoid are shopping malls, large grocery stores, or other places where quick escape is difficult.

For some, the fear of having a panic attack becomes so intense that the only solution is to rarely leave one's own home. This is known as panic disorder with concurrent *agoraphobia* (agoraphobia literally means an intense fear of public places). Regardless of the exact locales that might

Figure 2.3 The Flow of Panic Disorder

trigger panic for you, if you have panic disorder, panic attacks and the fear of having them greatly hinder your quality of life (see Figure 2.3).

SOCIAL ANXIETY DISORDER

Social anxiety disorder (SAD) refers to extreme anxiety of being seen and judged by others. If your SAD only rears its head in performance-related situations such as public speaking or other types of performing, you have the *performance-based subtype* of SAD. If, on the other hand, your social discomfort is experienced frequently in many social situations, you probably have SAD.

What distinguishes SAD from run-of-the-mill social anxiety is the intensity of the distress you experience. If you have SAD, you might feel painfully self-conscious about being seen or criticized by others when you are in the social settings that are particularly triggering for you. What's more, this anxiety quickly rises beyond the levels of mere discomfort. There are often accompanying physical components of SAD, such as having a racing heartbeat, blushing easily, feeling faint or dizzy, or perspiring excessively when you feel others looking at you. Similar to GAD, SAD has its own insidious cycle in which fear of being judged by others sparks a physical anxiety response, which in turn gives rise to worry that others will notice and judge the physical markers of your anxiety response. This cycle can go on ad infinitum, ramping up your anxiety levels.

If you have performance-based SAD only, this intense anxiety crops up in response to performance-based scenarios but does not inhibit you in other social settings. It's only human to experience some performance anxiety when you're about to go in front of a crowd or to experience some social anxiety in various social settings. However, with SAD, this anxiety is extreme.

David, a 20-year-old college student, suffered from SAD. He was doing well in school, had a few close friends, and had great relationships with his family back home. However, due to his SAD, living in the college dorms, attending classes, and eating in dining halls had become unbearable. Being around others in the dorms and dining halls was an almost constant source of agitation for David. He worried that he wouldn't know what to say if someone approached him, or that he would be judged by the others for being silent and awkward. Even when he sat alone to eat, David felt the eyes of others on him. If his two or three closest friends weren't around, he began getting carry-out meals and eating alone in his dorm room. David was also fearful that his SAD would affect his grades because it was agonizing for him to be part of group assignments. David was at the point of transferring to a community college so he could move home and be on campus as little as possible. Moving back home seemed like his only option.

Whether you struggle with SAD or performance-based SAD only, when confronted with this cycle of anxiety, the only solution in sight often is to avoid the anxiety-provoking social scenarios altogether. So, as with panic disorder and PTSD (described later), a significant component of social anxiety disorder is the avoidance of anxiety-triggering situations. This avoidance response can curtail social activities and interfere with your work or academic pursuits. And as with all anxiety disorders, rather than giving you relief, the avoidance behavior ends up maintaining your fears and sometimes intensifying your anxiety. The good news is that there are many more effective ways to alleviate your anxiety.

To summarize, SAD is characterized by the following symptoms:

— Intense fear of being seen and judged by others
— Physical symptoms: racing heart, feeling faint or dizzy (but not actually fainting), feeling hot or flushed, breaking out in a sweat that is caused by neither room temperature nor physical exertion
— Avoidance of social settings in which you might feel judged or under scrutiny
— One of two presentations: performance based, occurring only in response to specific social situations such as public speaking, or generalized, occurring in a broader range of social contexts

OBSESSIVE–COMPULSIVE DISORDER

Another disorder that creates runaway emotions is obsessive-compulsive disorder (OCD). As the name suggests, OCD is characterized by the presence of *obsessions* (recurrent, persistent, and intrusive thoughts, images, or urges) and/or *compulsions* (a set of actions or mental thought processes

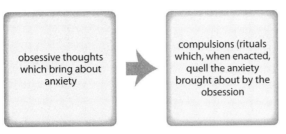

Figure 2.4 Two Main Components of Obsessive-Compulsive Disorder

you feel you must engage in to ward off harm or the distress brought about by the obsessive thought). (See Figure 2.4.)

If you have OCD, you may be plagued by a range of thoughts and behaviors that are contained under a big umbrella of distressing symptoms. Take, for instance, the folks in these examples who have different manifestations of OCD.

Debby has unrelenting, intrusive thoughts about germs and the fear that she or her children will be contaminated when they are away from home. She keeps away from people who are ill and spends an inordinate amount of time cleaning her home.

Johnny has a rigid routine of compulsive behaviors that he feels he must adhere to before he leaves the house. He checks and rechecks and rechecks the stove to make sure it is turned off and the doors and windows to make sure they are locked.

Elizabeth has a compulsion to repeat actions three times. She takes three paper towels to dry her hands in a public restroom. She chews her food three times on each side of her mouth, and when she goes on her daily runs, she has to run exactly three miles, no more and no less.

Some people with OCD have a need to touch or tap objects to diminish their anxiety. Typically the motivation for compulsive behaviors is related to the illusion that the compulsive action will prevent something bad from happening.

Others need reassurance from their physicians to whom they turn to frequently to quell their fears that something is seriously wrong with their health. Although their excessive concern about every symptom can seem like hypochondria to others, they can't stop the urge to get reassurance.

In the same family as OCD are disorders such as hoarding, *trichotillomania* (compulsive hair pulling), and *dermatillomania* (compulsive skin picking).

POSTTRAUMATIC STRESS DISORDER

If you have suffered a trauma, you are not alone. Surveys show that a majority of Americans experience at least one traumatic event during their lifetimes. Most recover fairly quickly and resume normal functioning, including many soldiers exposed to the violence of war. However, a multitude of people continue to suffer long after the traumatic event. These people have posttraumatic stress disorder (PTSD).

After serving in the army in Afghanistan, Alex entered therapy at the insistence of his wife, Julie. He was reluctant. He thought that seeking help meant he was weak and was convinced therapy wouldn't help. But when Julie said she'd leave the marriage if he didn't get professional help, he agreed. Although it was hard to talk about, Alex eventually shared that he had seen many people killed, including a close friend.

Alex suffered from classic symptoms of PTSD. He had difficulty falling asleep and staying asleep, and often wakened suddenly in a cold sweat following nightmares replaying the roadside bomb explosion that had sent a vehicle just ahead of his flying. He couldn't concentrate at work, especially because sudden sounds of horns and cars outside his office startled him. This was particularly severe when he heard tires screeching, just as his own vehicle had screeched to a stop after that explosion back in Afghanistan.

Often irritable, Alex began to lose his temper at his wife and young son over small annoyances. He said he just couldn't help having such a short fuse. Further, he was drinking excessively to take the edge off of his constant irritation and alarm.

Judy, age 60, was raped by her physician when she was 19. Although it was more than forty years ago, Judy said she felt as if the rape had happened yesterday. She had lost all sense of safety in the world. Indeed, she was always on edge, afraid to let her guard down.

Because of the rape, Judy couldn't tolerate many experiences that used to be normal. Annual checkups were out of the question. Doctors' visits occurred only for extreme emergencies. She avoided flying because the TSA screenings caused her immense distress. She felt panic and waves of nausea when the TSA employees performed a routine patdown. She recoiled in horror if anyone, including her husband, touched her in *just that way.*

PTSD develops following exposure to one or more traumatic events, such as sexual or physical assault, a natural disaster, exposure to war, witnessing harm done to another, or the unexpected injury or death of a loved one. Exposure to trauma does not necessarily lead to PTSD. One factor that is known to contribute to the development of PTSD is the person's *experience of* the trauma. The degree of helplessness the victim experiences can play a large role in whether or not PTSD develops.

There are four main symptoms associated with PTSD:

— *reliving of the traumatic event*: flashbacks, nightmares, or recurrent thoughts of the trauma
— *avoidance of stimuli reminiscent of the trauma*: avoiding places, sounds, and situations related to the trauma
— *emotional numbing*: detachment from others, a blunting of emotions, especially positive ones
— *heightened physiological arousal:* exaggerated startle responses, difficulty sleeping, irritability, poor concentration, hyperalertness

Survivors of trauma may be vulnerable to runaway, overwhelming emotions. Smells, sounds, or situations that are benign for others may be linked by association to the trauma and unleash a cascade of physical and emotional responses. Some people with PTSD experience dissociation and/or flashbacks. If you dissociate, you may detach from conscious awareness of the past or present trigger. The dissociation may protect you from the overwhelming distress of an event(s), but it may lead to feeling out of control and disoriented. People who have flashbacks reexperience the intense emotional and physical sensations of the actual trauma. These are usually very disturbing, interrupting your sleep and functioning.

DEPRESSION

As an advertisement for an antidepressant medication claims, "Depression hurts." People who suffer from depression can have an array of symptoms that include despondency, dejection, a lack of energy unrelated to lack of sleep, and difficulty experiencing pleasure. Depression impacts the nature of one's thoughts, which are often stuck on an endless loop of everything that is going wrong. Feelings of hopelessness and, for some, an extreme sense of guilt, persist.

Low energy, the tendency to ruminate on the negative, poor concentration, and social withdrawal are features of this disorder. Changes in appetite, sleep patterns, and muscle movements are common. While some people lose their appetites, others self-soothe with food, often with refined carbohydrates and sugar. Likewise, while some sleep excessively, others get too little sleep. Some depressed individuals become very jittery, sometimes having trouble sitting still, while others may feel like they're moving through molasses. Depression can literally alter the way that you walk through life.

Depression has been divided into categories based on its severity and duration. For example, major depressive disorder (MDD) is characterized by severe levels of depression. With MDD, depression can become so severe that it becomes difficult to work or take care of oneself or one's responsibilities. Thoughts of suicide can occur, and some in severe depression make plans for or actually attempt suicide.

Marianne reported to her physician at her annual exam that it was getting increasingly difficult for her to get out of bed in the morning. "All I want to do is sleep, and I resent having to do anything—like work—that generally interrupts my rest. What's crazy, too, is that despite how much time I spend in bed, I still feel tired. I feel like I have to drag myself everywhere."

Marianne said she had lost 20 pounds in the last 2 months. She explained, "Food holds no interest for me anymore. I don't seem to look forward to anything and eating just happens to fall into that category. It takes too much energy to cook anything. And I don't want to go out to eat. Aside from the effort of going somewhere, I hate going out to eat alone—and there's no way I'd call any of my friends to join me. They wouldn't want to be around me when I'm like this—who would?"

If you have MDD, you might experience depression episodically. That is, the depression waxes and wanes, and you might be in a deep depression for, say, 2 weeks or 2 months, and then have a long break in symptoms before the next depression sets in. On the other hand, some people might have only one episode and once the fog of depression lifts, the depression is truly over.

There are, however, less severe forms of depression than MDD. For example, a diagnosis that used to be known only as *dysthymia* (this now falls under the category of *persistent depressive disorder*, or PDD) is given if you are mildly depressed for most of the day, more days than not, over a sustained, lengthy amount of time. This low-grade depression has to have persisted for at least 2 years for an adult to be diagnosed with PDD. While the depression never gets as severe as MDD, this lower level, sustained depression still takes a harsh toll. While the recurring episodes of MDD can be likened to coming in seasons, persistent, low-grade depression is a long, bleak winter that does not let up.

Sally, a 55-year-old, divorced attorney, used to meet her law school friends 3 days a week at the gym to work out. Sometimes they would go out for an early dinner afterward. For over a year, however, Sally had missed her exercise classes. At first her friends had called, asking if she wanted to meet them after their workout for dinner. But after a few months, they stopped calling. Returning their calls and getting to the gym took too much effort for Sally. When pressed, she said that life had seemed bleak for quite some time. She still functioned well at work, and she doubted that her clients and colleagues detected changes in her performance. But for a very long time, she had been living life in black and white rather than in color. She just couldn't seem to find the momentum to get back what she had lost and didn't understand how or why the color in her life had faded away.

The behaviors that might lessen depression, including exercise, social interactions, and accomplishing goals, feel almost impossible to the depressed person. Nonetheless, any positive action is a step in a good direction. Using the tools offered in this workbook helps modulate feelings of sadness and hopelessness and lessens feelings of loneliness and isolation.

DEPRESSION AND ANXIETY TOGETHER

It is not uncommon for people to have both depression and an anxiety disorder. This is often referred to as a "comorbid" disorder. The unrelenting, discouraging nature of anxiety disorders can lead to chronic despair and hopelessness—two signposts of depression. However, comorbid anxiety and depression can develop in other patterns. Brain research shows that anxiety and depression have common neurological underpinnings. For instance, both disorders show irregularities in the production or functioning of some of the same neurotransmitters, such as serotonin. This helps to explain why some of the same medications can be used to successfully treat both depressive and anxious symptoms. Certain research indicates there might be a genetic link as well.

INTERMITTENT EXPLOSIVE DISORDER

This disorder is characterized by frequent angry outbursts, including verbal tirades, tantrums, or other explosive or aggressive behavior. Typically, the "explosions" are impulsive reactions that the individual feels are provoked by a situation or person. The reaction is an overreaction, the intensity of which is markedly out of proportion to the aggravating stressor. Intermittent explosive disorder (IED) is often expressed in road rage or violent interchanges with spouses or coworkers. At times, the emotional reaction is so intense that the explosive individual physically hurts someone or destroys property.

People vulnerable to this disorder often have a history of physical and emotional trauma in childhood and adolescence. But a trauma history by no means guarantees development of IED. If you suffer from depression, anxiety, or substance abuse disorders, you also may be more vulnerable to developing IED. The intense, angry outbursts associated with IED occur whether the person is intoxicated or sober. However, a person who becomes angry and/or violent *only* when drunk would not be diagnosed with IED.

Eric, 26, was close to losing his job after three inappropriate outbursts of anger at the workplace. Once, he shouted insults at a delivery man who had set a heavy package on his desk rather than the table. Another time, he lost his temper when a colleague accidentally bumped into him in the break room. What topped off the incidents and put him on probation occurred during his performance review, when he ripped up the documents and stormed out of the room. He felt remorse over the outbursts but feared he would lose control again.

Life at home was even worse. Due to his inability to keep a job, Eric had been living in his mother's house to save money. Even there his outbursts of anger occurred about twice a week. Finally his mother told him to move out when she couldn't tolerate his explosive anger.

Some people with IED take their rage out on other people physically. If this is something you do, it is essential that you use the tools in this workbook to better modulate your emotion, as your anger can have a significant, negative impact on both yourself and those around you.

Take-Away Points

— Everyone experiences an ever-changing, constant flow of emotions.

— The goal is to modulate the intensity of your emotion, not eradicate it.

— Your ability to experience emotion enriches and enhances your experience of life. However, when you experience emotional flooding and have no tools to ease it, you experience great suffering.

— Emotional flooding plays a key role in *all* psychological disorders.

— In addition to using the tools in this workbook, if you have a psychological disorder, you might also benefit from professional counseling.

3 Conflicts in Relationships

Fire can warm or consume, water can quench or drown, wind can caress or cut. And so it is with human relationships: we can both create and destroy, nurture and terrorize, traumatize and heal each other.

—BRUCE PERRY AND MAIA SZALAVITZ

RELATIONSHIPS ARE AN INTEGRAL PART OF HUMAN EXISTENCE. YOUR MOST intimate relationships provide joy, meaning, substance, support, and solace in your life. Interacting with friends, acquaintances, and coworkers also gives you numerous opportunities for meaningful connection. Even exchanges with the many strangers that you encounter on any given day—the barista making your latte, the mail carrier bringing you a delivery—can offer moments of connection if you're willing to offer a smile, a thank-you, or exchange a few words of light conversation.

Yet if you interact with people, conflict is a given. Runaway emotions rear their ugly heads when you deal with your romantic partners, your children (both when they are young *and* grown), your parents, your siblings, your friends, your coworkers—even people you don't personally know but simply encounter during routine daily activities.

In response to your interactions with other people, you may, at times, feel:

— abandoned
— betrayed
— controlled
— criticized

— judged/shamed

— misunderstood

— resentful

— defeated/helpless

These feelings, in turn, can trigger emotional flooding.

Relationships can be as challenging as they are rewarding. But when emotional flooding enters the picture, the intensity of challenges grows and the rewards markedly lessen. This, however, doesn't need to be the case. In this chapter you gain insight into the relationship dynamics that trigger and perpetuate emotional flooding. With this information you then begin identifying the ways you are frequently triggered in your relationships.

First, it is important to understand why shared connection is so powerful and its absence so painful.

The Importance of Attuned Connection

Humans are social beings. Your experience of connection provides you with love, nurturance, and support. Connection is fundamental to your ability to survive and thrive. Particularly, a specific type of connection called *attuned connection* is crucial. Your need for experiences of attuned connection begins in infancy and continues throughout your entire life.

Two people experience *attuned connection* when they are resonating emotionally and are on the same emotional page. This occurs through spoken words, nonverbal communication, and responsive attention. When you and another person experience attuned connection, emotion-based centers in your brains fire in similar patterns. As we wrote in *Anxious in Love*, attuned connection can give you a wonderful feeling that "emotionally [you] are humming the same tune" (Daitch & Lorberbaum, 2012, p. 97). The language of attuned connection encompasses:

— receptive, soothing touch

— shared glances

— reciprocal body language

— shared experiences of happiness, joy, and contentment

— soothing responses to sorrow or distress

THE NEUROSCIENCE OF CONNECTION

Recall from Chapter 1 that when you are flooded with emotion, your midbrain (responsible for emotion) becomes highly activated. When this occurs, communication between your midbrain and your forebrain is interrupted and the midbrain takes center stage. You learned that this disconnect blocks the midbrain from "hearing" the rational, logic-based input from your forebrain: You are cut off from the part of yourself that can listen to reason. When the midbrain goes rogue, there is a second consequence of the neurological disconnect that can be equally detrimental: You are cut off from the ability to experience attuned connection with others.

EMOTIONAL FLOODING AND RUPTURES IN ATTUNED CONNECTION

Because the presence of an attuned other is calming and soothing when you are upset, it's natural to seek the care of such a person when you're emotionally flooded—even when a relationship trigger has sent you into emotional flooding to begin with. However, without the ability to calm your own flooding with the tools in this workbook, this often leads to the escalation of conflict rather than the dissolution of it.

Attunement with another requires a balance of forebrain and midbrain activity (Siegel, 2007) that is disrupted when your midbrain, the control center of your emotions, goes rogue and the rational forebrain speaks with all the grabbing power of a whisper. That's why, when you become flooded with emotion, you are unable to experience attuned connection. With emotional flooding dominating you, even the most caring, receptive friend or family member may not be able to give you the sense of attuned connection and well-being that you want. So you're likely to feel further frustrated, disparaged, or hurt. And since your rational forebrain is not in charge at the moment, you may easily blame the rift in connection on the other person: If this person *really* cared about you, her attempts to provide you with comfort would work. Given your emotional flooding, you are unable to heed the input of both your own logical forebrain *and* input from the rational forebrains of others.

The following chart shows the specific losses that result from ruptures in connection and emotional flooding.

Emotional Flooding and Ruptures in Attuned Connection			
Unable to Feel		**Unable to "Hear"**	
FROM SELF:	FROM OTHERS:	FROM SELF:	FROM OTHERS:
Ease	Care	Logic-based attempts to "talk yourself down" or calm your emotions	Logic-based attempts to "talk you down" or calm your emotions
Well-being	Supportiveness		
Soothing	Soothing		
Comfort	Comfort		

The chart illustrates why it is essential to get your emotional flooding in check by engaging the tools you will learn in Part II *before* seeking support from others. While you are highly flooded, the care, support, and soothing that is offered to you most likely won't sink in. What's worse, your disappointment at not receiving what you yearn for may escalate the flooding. It can also leave the other person feeling powerless when the support or logic-based solutions are not taken in. This dynamic, in turn, can cause conflict to grow with both participants feeling alone in a sea of emotions—that keeps you both from being able to connect with one another.

EMOTIONAL FLOODING: DEFENSIVENESS AND WITHDRAWAL

When you become dysregulated during interactions with others and emotional flooding occurs, your emotions often dictate the way you interact. And interactions governed by emotional flooding lead to two common reactions:

1. Defensiveness: characterized by counterattacks toward the other person.
   These can take the form of
   - criticizing
   - blaming
   - belittling

- mocking
- making a laundry list of the other person's faults
- bringing up past arguments or incidents

2. **Withdrawal:** characterized by refusing contact with the other person. This can take the form of
   - giving the silent treatment
   - sulking
   - leaving and refusing to come back for a period of time

NOTE: *withdrawal* in this context differs from taking a break for a time-out. With withdrawal, the distance serves to widen the disconnect. A time-out, on the other hand, is a pause in contact that serves to facilitate connection upon your return.

In summary, emotional flooding, if unchecked, can:

— block your ability to feel connection with others
— block others' ability to connect with you
— block the negotiation of conflict
— lead to the unnecessary escalation of conflict and dissolution of relationships due to defensiveness or withdrawal

RECOGNIZING YOUR DEFENSIVENESS AND WITHDRAWAL

Use the following list to identify the characteristic ways you behave when you're emotionally flooded. Place a checkmark in the boxes indicating your most frequents reactions.

Defensiveness: characterized by various types of counterattacks toward the other person.

Check the box(es) of the form of defensiveness you engage in:

☐ Criticizing
☐ Blaming
☐ Belittling
☐ Mocking
☐ Making a laundry list of the other person's faults
☐ Bringing up past arguments or incidents
☐ Other _____

Withdrawal: characterized by various ways of refusing contact with the other person.

Check the box(es) of the form of withdrawal you typically engage in:

☐ giving the silent treatment (trying to punish the other person by refusing to talk)

☐ sulking

☐ storming out of the room, house, or general area, and refusing to come back for a period of time

☐ Other _____

USING THE TOOLS TO CREATE CHANGE

When flooding occurs in a relationship, it is essential to apply the tools you'll learn in Part II immediately, because the experience of emotional flooding blocks you from being able to experience attuned connection. Your application of the tools is not just in service to you, but to the others in relationship with you. When you engage the tools to regulate your emotion, you are able to bring your rational forebrain back online.

Identifying Your Susceptibility to Emotional Flooding in Relationships

Now that you have a road map of how emotional flooding disrupts connection and causes destruction, it is time to start learning how to intervene when flooding occurs. The first step in this process involves getting a clear understanding of the triggers you are particularly sensitive to, and how they emerge for you in various relationships. In Part II, Chapter 8, you will learn to address these triggers when they emerge.

INFLUENCE OF EARLY ENVIRONMENT

In order to better understand the ways that you are susceptible to emotional flooding in the present, it is crucial to understand how you have been sensitized to certain triggers as a result of past experiences. You gain a better sense of who you are today by thoroughly recognizing the impact of your early relationships.

Like everyone, you learn what to expect in the future based on what you have experienced in the past. For example, you learn that when the sun begins to lower in the sky, it will soon set, darkness will come, and the temperature will cool. Because the sun rises and sets each day, you know what to expect as each 24-hour cycle revolves. By noticing the patterns in your environment, you can adapt accordingly.

"In every conceivable manner, the family is link to our past, bridge to our future."
—ALEX HALEY

TEMPLATES AND GENERALIZATIONS

From past experience, you can form a template with which to view and interact with the world around you. Likewise, you form a template of what to expect in relationships with others, based on your experiences with your parents, siblings, extended family, and community. You use these templates by generalizing, sometimes inaccurately, past learning to new relationships.

As a child you might have learned that your father was usually grumpy when he first got home from work, but after having some time to unwind, he was good natured. So you might have adapted to his mood accordingly, leaving him alone for a while before trying to get his attention. When you're young, you unconsciously develop strategies to adapt to the emotional environment of the family—their expectations, criticisms, and praise. As an adult, you often generalize these strategies to your interactions with others.

The problem is that it's not always easy to recognize the childhood strategies that you carry into your present relationships. The result is that they distort your perceptions, dictate your behavior, and may cause unnecessary suffering. As an adult, when you are emotionally triggered in relationships, it is important to ask yourself if your reaction is based on childhood coping strategies. If it is, remind yourself that these strategies are antiquated and no longer necessary in your adult relationships. This conscious awareness makes it easier to navigate your relationships, making you less vulnerable to emotional flooding.

"The unconscious mind seems to have no sense of linear time . . . our unfinished business with our early caretakers becomes a compelling agenda [in our adult relationships]."
— HARVILLE HENDRIX AND HELEN LAKELLY HUNT

Judy found that she became anxious whenever she needed to confront her husband about something bothering her. In therapy, she became aware that her father was particularly intolerant of any criticism. Whenever her mother attempted to confront him, he overreacted to what he perceived as criticism and vehemently counterattacked, often bringing his wife to tears. Judy learned that confrontation was emotionally unsafe. The problem was that rather than concluding that her father, in particular, reacted negatively to criticism, Judy unconsciously generalized her learning to a fear of confronting anyone in her life. She avoided making complaints, asserting herself, and speaking up. Her heightened emotional response in the past had been adaptive, but as an adult it was detrimental to her functioning.

The following chart gives examples of childhood dynamics in the home, the overgeneralizations that can arise from them, the cost of these childhood lessons, and beneficial reevaluations after recognizing the pattern.

Early Environment	Overgeneralization	Result	Current Reevaluation
My parents fought all the time.	Marriages are full of conflict. I will not get married.	I become prone to emotional flooding when a boyfriend talks about marriage.	My parents' unhappy marriage doesn't mean I will have an unhappy marriage.
Mother is highly judgmental when I make mistakes.	Making mistakes is not okay. When I make a mistake, I will be harshly judged.	I become prone to emotional flooding after making a mistake.	My mother judged mistakes harshly, but not all people do. And if they do, that doesn't have to reflect on me.
Mother is very focused on my appearance.	I must look beautiful in order to be accepted.	I become prone to emotional flooding when I think others are judging the way I look.	I am acceptable based on who I am, not just on how I look.

The common saying, "If I'm hysterical, it's probably historical" reflects the reality that sometimes when you are very upset, the degree of flooding is highly influenced by your history.

INFLUENCE OF EARLY ENVIRONMENT: EXERCISES

To better regulate your emotional flooding, it is key to get a sense of what types of interpersonal triggers result from your early life experience. The following exercises help you discover when childhood patterns are fueling emotional flooding in your current interactions.

SELF-ASSESSMENT OF EMOTIONAL TRIGGERS
BASED ON EARLY ENVIRONMENT

In my childhood home,

I felt	Never	Rarely	Sometimes	Frequently	Almost Always
☐ abandoned	1	2	3	4	5
☐ betrayed	1	2	3	4	5
☐ controlled	1	2	3	4	5
☐ criticized	1	2	3	4	5
☐ lack of empathy	1	2	3	4	5
☐ judged/shamed	1	2	3	4	5
☐ betrayed	1	2	3	4	5
☐ misunderstood	1	2	3	4	5
☐ resentful	1	2	3	4	5
☐ defeated/hopeless	1	2	3	4	5

If you circled a 4 or 5 for any of these, put a check in the box next to that feeling. This is one of your triggers. When you begin to feel emotionally flooded, you need to be mindful of how your current reactions are mirroring past emotional patterns. Completing the chart that follows using your triggers and childhood experience can help you achieve this mindfulness.

Early Environment	Overgeneralization	Fallout	Current Reevaluation

IDENTIFYING TRIGGERS IN RELATIONSHIPS

Although challenges are inevitable in relationships, emotional flooding is not. Next you can identify the types of interactions in which your emotional flooding most frequently surfaces. In some cases, this flooding may be directly linked to generalizations from reactions you learned from your early environment. In others, you may be reactive for different reasons. The key is to gain awareness of the relationships that trigger you today. With this knowledge, you will be better prepared to stop an overreaction before it causes flooding.

Although your intimate relationships, such as with your partners or children or parents, are the most likely to elicit emotional flooding, the full range of types of relationships and interactions, including those that follow, can have that effect:

- Romantic
- Parent–child
- Parent–adult child
- Sibling
- In-law
- Close friend
- Romantic partner's friend
- Coworkers
- Acquaintances
- Service providers
- Anonymous passersby (other drivers on the road, the person next to you in line, etc.)

In the inventory that follows, circle the appropriate number in response to the following statement next to each relationship.

I experience emotional flooding in the following relationships:

	Never	Rarely	Sometimes	Frequently	Almost Always
romantic partner	1	2	3	4	5
young child/children	1	2	3	4	5
adult child/children	1	2	3	4	5
mother	1	2	3	4	5
father	1	2	3	4	5
step-parent(s)	1	2	3	4	5
sister(s)	1	2	3	4	5
brother(s)	1	2	3	4	5
in-laws	1	2	3	4	5
close friend(s)	1	2	3	4	5
peripheral friend(s)	1	2	3	4	5
partner's friends	1	2	3	4	5
boss/supervisor	1	2	3	4	5
supervisees	1	2	3	4	5
colleagues	1	2	3	4	5
acquaintances	1	2	3	4	5

service providers	1	2	3	4	5
anonymous passersby	1	2	3	4	5

From this list of relationships, make a list of the people who trigger emotional flooding at a level of 4 or 5. Then you will complete the following exercises for each person on your list.

PEOPLE WHO TRIGGER EMOTIONAL FLOODING (LEVEL 4 OR 5) ━━━━━━━━━━

1. _____
2. _____
3. _____
4. _____
5. _____

Next, complete the checklist and tables that follow for each person on your list. (If you run out of room in the space provided here, additional checklists and tables can be found in Appendix C.)

In the inventory that follows, circle the appropriate number for each emotion possibly causing flooding.

In my relationship with _____.

I feel	Never	Rarely	Sometimes	Frequently	Almost Always
abandoned	1	2	3	4	5
betrayed	1	2	3	4	5
controlled	1	2	3	4	5
criticized	1	2	3	4	5
judged/shamed	1	2	3	4	5
betrayed	1	2	3	4	5
misunderstood	1	2	3	4	5
lack of empathy	1	2	3	4	5
resentment	1	2	3	4	5
defeated/helpless	1	2	3	4	5

For any trigger for which you circled a 4 or 5, fill in the following tables. If there were more than three such triggers, continue writing on a separate sheet of paper. In addition, if there is a trigger that does not occur often but is highly painful when it does occur, add it to the table that follows.

Trigger	Painful Thoughts and Feelings That Come Up in Response

Often following painful thoughts and feelings in response to a trigger, you might react by becoming defensive or withdrawing. (See List of Behaviors, p. 40–41)

For the same triggers you entered in the earlier chart, describe your defensive or withdrawing behavior.

Trigger	Ways in Which I Become Defensive and/or Withdraw

In my relationship with _____.

I feel	Never	Rarely	Sometimes	Frequently	Almost Always
abandoned	1	2	3	4	5
betrayed	1	2	3	4	5
controlled	1	2	3	4	5
criticized	1	2	3	4	5
judged/shamed	1	2	3	4	5
betrayed	1	2	3	4	5
misunderstood	1	2	3	4	5
lack of empathy	1	2	3	4	5
resentment	1	2	3	4	5
defeated/helpless	1	2	3	4	5

For any trigger in which you circled a 4 or 5, fill in the following tables. If there were more than three triggers that meet these criteria, continue writing on a separate sheet of paper. In addition, if there is a trigger that does not occur often in this relationship but is highly painful the few times that it does occur, add it to the table that follows.

Trigger	Painful Thoughts and Feelings That Come Up in Response

For the same triggers you entered in the chart, describe your defensive or withdrawing behavior. (See List of Behaviors, p. 40–41)

Trigger	Ways in Which I Become Defensive and/or Withdraw

In my relationship with _____.

I feel	Never	Rarely	Sometimes	Frequently	Almost Always
abandoned	1	2	3	4	5
betrayed	1	2	3	4	5
controlled	1	2	3	4	5
criticized	1	2	3	4	5
judged/shamed	1	2	3	4	5
betrayed	1	2	3	4	5
misunderstood	1	2	3	4	5
lack of empathy	1	2	3	4	5
resentment	1	2	3	4	5
defeated/helpless	1	2	3	4	5

For any trigger in which you circled a 4 or 5, fill in the following tables. If there were more than three triggers that meet this criteria, continue writing on a separate sheet of paper. In addition, if there is a trigger that does not occur often in this relationship but is highly detrimental when it does occur, add it to the following table.

Trigger	Painful Thoughts and Feelings That Come Up in Response

For the same triggers you entered in the chart, describe your defensive or withdrawing behavior. (See List of Behaviors, p. 40-41)

Trigger	Ways in Which I Become Defensive and/or Withdraw

In my relationship with _____.

I feel	Never	Rarely	Sometimes	Frequently	Almost Always
abandoned	1	2	3	4	5
betrayed	1	2	3	4	5
controlled	1	2	3	4	5
criticized	1	2	3	4	5
judged/shamed	1	2	3	4	5
betrayed	1	2	3	4	5
misunderstood	1	2	3	4	5

lack of empathy	1	2	3	4	5
resentment	1	2	3	4	5
defeated/helpless	1	2	3	4	5

For any trigger in which you circled a 4 or 5, fill in the following tables. If there were more than three triggers that meet these criteria, continue writing on a separate sheet of paper. In addition, if there is a trigger that does not occur often in this relationship but is highly detrimental the few times that it does crop up, add it to the following table.

Trigger	Painful Thoughts and Feelings That Come Up in Response

For the same triggers you entered in the chart, describe your defensive or withdrawing behavior. (See List of Behaviors, p. 40-41)

Trigger	Ways in Which I Become Defensive and/or Withdraw

Take-Away Points

— Interpersonal interactions, whether with your closest family members or complete strangers, can trigger emotional flooding.

— When the midbrain goes rogue, you are cut off from the ability to experience connection with others. In other words, when you become flooded with emotion, your ability to experience attuned connection is blocked.

— It is essential to engage the tools you will learn in Part II to get your own emotional flooding in check *before* seeking support from others. If you seek support from others while you are flooded, the care, support, and soothing that is offered most likely won't be able to sink in.

— You form a template of what you can expect in relationships with others based on your experiences of interactions in your childhood environment with parents, other caretakers, siblings, and extended family.

— Overreactions in the present can be determined by those experiences in your past that remain unrecognized.

— By engaging the tools you will learn you are acting in the best interests of your relationships as well as yourself.

PART II

The Road to Self-Regulation

4 The Daily Stress Inoculation

*Do you have the patience to wait
'til your mind settles and the water is clear?*
—TAO TE CHING

A KEY TO SUCCESSFULLY LESSENING YOUR EMOTIONAL FLOODING IS TO IMPLE-
ment and repeatedly use a structured, easy program we call the Daily
Stress Inoculation (DSI). The DSI is a daily practice that diminishes your
baseline levels of tension and anxiety and, thus, your overall reactivity.
With the Daily Stress Inoculation, you have the tools to enhance your sense
of resiliency and calm throughout your day. In doing so, you decrease the
emotional flooding and relationship conflicts that can otherwise ensue
when your baseline stress levels are higher. However, those changes don't
happen just because you recognize that the DSI is good for you. Therefore,
this chapter also provides strategies that will help you implement the DSI
on a regular basis.

Benefits of the Daily Stress Inoculation

Teaching your mind and body to gear down has four major benefits: bal-
ancing the autonomic nervous system, recalibrating stress-hormone levels,
producing optimal brain-wave activity, and enhancing the effectiveness of
the time-outs you will learn.

BALANCING THE AUTONOMIC NERVOUS SYSTEM

The autonomic nervous system is composed of three branches, two of which, the *sympathetic* and *parasympathetic*, are pertinent to our discussion. The sympathetic and parasympathetic nervous systems can be thought of as counterparts that complement one another in their respective roles. The sympathetic nervous system (SNS) acts as a "gas pedal," telling your system to rev up during times when you need to take action to defend your safety. It is the branch of the nervous system that mobilizes you into fight or flight when you are under threat. Activation of the SNS can quicken your heartbeat, release hormones such as norepinephrine to energize you, and make sure that muscle groups that assist in physical action (associated with fighting or fleeing) are oxygenated and energized. When the SNS is in full swing, you are revved, highly alert, and ready to respond with a hair trigger to the environment around you (see Figure 4.1).

The parasympathetic nervous system (PNS) acts as the "brake pedal" to the revving of the SNS. It wouldn't be safe to step on the gas unless your body also had the ability to brake and slow yourself down. Ideally, the PNS engages to calm the revving of the SNS when the call to arms is no longer needed. The PNS does this by releasing neurotransmitters targeted to calm the body down, such as slowing the heart rate and reinstating regular digestive activity, which is halted during SNS activation when energy is diverted to mobilize for defensive action. PNS activation sends the body the message that it's okay to relax again. It helps everything from your skeletal

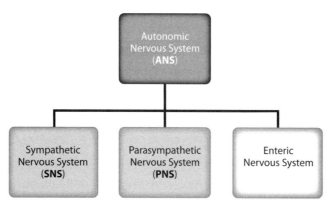

Figure 4.1 The Autonomic Nervous System

muscles to your heart rate settle back into a state of relaxation, promoting a sense of calm and ease.

When you're prone to emotional flooding, however, the sympathetic nervous system can become chronically hyperactive. The SNS remains overengaged and the PNS doesn't adequately apply the brakes. In essence, you're running on high alert and are more prone to respond with a hair trigger as you go about your day. Psychophysiologically, you're setting yourself up for emotional flooding to occur.

In addition, physiological fallout can result from heightened SNS activity. Some people with chronically hyperactive SNS activation can experience physical discomforts such as frequent stomach upsets or other gastrointestinal distress, muscle aches, and tension headaches. This is especially the case when chronic SNS activation is a component of an anxiety disorder such as generalized anxiety disorder or posttraumatic stress disorder. When the PNS doesn't kick in to apply the brakes and create states of calm and relaxation, your whole being—body and psyche—suffers.

By using the Daily Stress Inoculation, you're training your parasympathetic nervous system to apply those brakes. In essence, you're greasing the breaks and fine-tuning the PNS-ANS engine so that the two counterparts can complement one another optimally once again.

RECALIBRATING STRESS-HORMONE LEVELS

Another negative outcome associated with chronically heightened sympathetic nervous system activation involves stress hormone levels. Recall that when the SNS kicks in, hormones such as norepinephrine are released. These hormones act as chemical messengers that help gear the body up for action. When the SNS is chronically hyperactive, elevated levels of these stress hormones circulate throughout the body. This can add to the sense of having a hair trigger, leaving you feeling more keyed up, anxious, and prone to emotional flooding. In addition, elevated levels of stress hormones contribute to the physical discomforts associated with chronic SNS activation mentioned earlier, such as gastrointestinal upsets and pains resulting from chronic muscle tension.

By helping you optimize the interplay of SNS-PNS activation, the DSI helps decrease the amount of stress hormones released into your system.

Simultaneously, the DSI helps increase the presence of protective neuro-chemicals such as serotonin, a neurochemical linked to positive mood. As we noted in our book *Anxious in Love* (Daitch & Lorberbaum, 2012), when you engage daily in a calming practice, you shift your internal homeostasis. Just as your body temperature stays at about 98 degrees, incorporating the DSI into your regular routine regulates your internal homeostasis by lowering your baseline stress temperature. By practicing the DSI you can actually alter the balance of neurochemicals released into your system.

FOSTERING OPTIMAL BRAIN-WAVE ACTIVITY

Regular practice of the DSI can also stimulate brain-wave patterns associated with states of calm and relaxation. Brain waves are created as the millions of cells in your brain communicate with one another. This communication is facilitated by the presence of small electric currents. This electrical activity in the cells of the brain displays wave-like patterns that differ according to particular states of mind. For example, beta waves are associated with stress, anxiety, and worry. Alpha and theta waves, on the other hand, are associated with calmness and relaxation.

If you experience chronic SNS activation, you are most likely generating a flurry of beta-wave activity. By engaging in the DSI, you give your brain the opportunity to shift into alpha and theta rhythms. You are, in essence, helping the cells in your brain march to the beat of a different drummer.

The Daily Stress Inoculation

The Daily Stress Inoculation (DSI) has five components:

— Focusing attention with the *Eye Roll*
— Releasing tension with *Tight Fist*
— Relaxing the nervous system with *Focusing on the Breath*
— Deepening relaxation with *Safe Place*
— Reinforcing your effort and success with *Closing Affirmations*

LEARNING THE DAILY STRESS INOCULATION

Eye Roll

PURPOSE
— Interrupt the intensity of physical and emotional reactions
— Focus attention
— Increase responsiveness to positive suggestions

The Eye Roll is inspired by the research of Dr. Herbert Spiegel, a professor of psychiatry and a leader in the field of clinical hypnosis. Spiegel initially used this technique to assess a person's capacity for being hypnotized (Spiegel, 1972). It is also a great way to quickly focus attention and stop heightening emotion (Daitch, 2007).

The Eye Roll can be done with your eyes open or closed. If you wish to use this technique discreetly when other people are nearby, you can choose to use the closed-eye version. This option makes it useful as a quick de-stressing technique without taking a formal time-out.

A small percentage of people find the Eye Roll uncomfortable because of the tensing in the eye muscles. While this sense of tension is perfectly normal, if you find it too uncomfortable, you can reduce the degree to which you gaze upward.

DIRECTIONS
1. Roll your eyes upward as if you are trying to look at the centermost point in the arch of each of your eyebrows.
2. As you roll your eyes upward, also take in a slow, deep breath.
3. Hold your eyes gazing upward while holding the breath for a few seconds before relaxing your eyes and exhaling, allowing your eyes to drift back to their original position.

Tight Fist

PURPOSE
— Quickly release muscular tension
— Quickly discharge stress, anxiety, fear, worry, anger, and frustration

The Tight Fist technique literally helps you calm down by tensing up. When you're revving into an overreaction, one of the hardest things to do is to calm down. Like Newton's law of physics, an object in motion tends to stay in motion. When you're heading into an overreaction, it's hard to halt that overreaction in its tracks. It's even harder to turn your trajectory in the opposite direction, that is, calming down rather than revving up. The Tight Fist technique draws on the natural tendency to tense the body when you're distressed. One way to relax the muscles is to first accentuate that tension. The Tight Fist exercise accumulates the tension from the entire body into one fist and then releases it, thereby eliciting a relaxation response. Next, this exercise harnesses the power of visualization to make the experience more powerful. The accompanying audio track guides you to clench and hold your fist and then visualize the tension and stress exiting your body as you release your clenched fist.

DIRECTIONS

1. Imagine that all your worry, fear, and muscular tension are going into your dominant hand.
2. Make a fist with that hand, squeeze it tightly, feel the tension.
3. Magnify it, and tighten that fist even more, tighter and tighter.
4. Imagine that tension becoming a liquid in a color of your choice; the liquid represents your distress, worry, any uncomfortable feeling in your body.
5. Imagine your fist absorbing all of the colored liquid, all the fear, all the discomfort.
6. Release your fist slowly, one finger at a time, and imagine the colored liquid flowing to the floor and through the floor to the ground, to be absorbed deep into the soil.
7. You can repeat squeezing your fist and releasing the liquid again, noticing the difference between tension and relaxation.
8. Repeat the exercise with your nondominant hand.

Focusing on the Breath

"Feelings come and go like clouds in a windy sky. Conscious breathing is my anchor."

—THICH NHAT HANH

PURPOSE
— Engage self-soothing
— Elicit relaxation
— Divert attention from distressing thoughts, emotions, or physical sensations

Attending to the breath and slowing down your respiration rate is a simple but highly effective way to calm the nervous system. While rapid breathing is associated with increased tension and anxiety reactions, slow breathing is associated with emotional equilibrium.

There are a number of ways to breathe away tension. It can be as simple as gently observing your breath without the need to alter it. The attending process in itself typically serves to slow the respiration rate, although that is not the only goal.

In addition, it diverts attention from distressing thoughts, emotions, or sensations and activates the calming parasympathetic nervous system.

DIRECTIONS
1. Observe your breathing without trying to change it.
2. Notice the temperature, rhythm, and pace of your breath.
3. Think the word "comfort" with each inhalation and the word "relax" with each exhalation.
4. Let yourself experience the sensation of floating as you breathe in and out.
5. Notice the relief that comes from observing the breath.

PRACTICING THE FIRST THREE TECHNIQUES
Now that you have familiarized yourself with the first three techniques in the DSI, you are ready to practice them using Track 2 of the audio recording that accompanies this workbook. Find a comfortable, quiet space, sit back, and enjoy your first run-through of the Eye Roll, Tight Fist, and Focusing

on the Breath. After you have listened to the track once or twice, you can then proceed to learning the next DSI component, Safe Place.

Creating Your Safe Place

PURPOSE

— Provide comfort and interrupt the reactive mind.

— Provide an easily accessed set of positive, relaxing, and comforting feelings that you can return to as needed.

— Imagine an environment or container in which you can feel safe.

— Enhance a sense of self-confidence, control, or empowerment that comes from using your imagination to experience an ideal environment.

The following exercise teaches you to create your safe place, which you will return to daily during your daily stress inoculation. In creating your safe place you will also be guided to create a cue that will allow you to quickly invoke all the sights, smells, sounds, and imagery of your safe place, making it easier to quickly access your safe place whenever you wish.

Your ideal, go-to safe place might surprise you and might be different on any given day. There are many different reasons that one safe place might feel like a "best fit" on a particular day, and another safe place might feel like a best fit on the next. On the other hand, you might prefer the consistency of returning to the same safe place each day. Feel free to create multiple safe places and to re-envision your safe place(s) as often as you wish. The only wrong way to do this is by not doing it at all.

Creating a safe place requires imagination and visualization to help you access a calm, serene state in which you experience a strong sense of relaxation and well-being. By imagining being in a soothing place, you can quickly shift your body and mind to this state. The key to successful visualization is incorporating all the senses. The more details you include of what you see, hear, smell, and feel in your safe place, the more real it feels. And the more real it feels, the better. While your safe place exists in your mind, by enlivening all your senses you actually invoke the experience in the present moment.

DIRECTIONS

1. Focus your entire attention on developing an image of a warm and welcoming safe place. This can be a place you remember or one that you're creating in your imagination.

2. Imagine all the sensory details of this place:
   - Sights (colors, shapes, hues, lighting, etc.)
   - Sounds (wind, surf, running water, birds, etc.)
   - Smells (fragrances, scents, aromas, etc.)
   - Tactile sensations (temperature, what's under your feet or supporting your body, whether you're sitting, lying, standing, or walking, etc.)

3. Select a verbal cue or visual cue to remind you of your safe place and bring back the feeling of comfort you associate with it. For example, your cue might be the phrase "ocean of blue" or a symbol might be a sailboat.

Now that you've familiarized yourself with the steps for creating your safe place, get comfortable, prepare to relax, and play audio Track 3 to create your new place.

(From Norton's *Anxiety Disorders: The Go-To Guide for Clients and Therapists* [Daitch, 2011]).

Closing Affirmations

PURPOSE

— Harness the power of your words.

— Recognize and reaffirm that you are taking daily action to lower your baseline stress temperature.

— Identify and engage thoughts that bring about empowerment.

Words have power. Positive affirmations, which we'll refer to as *self-statements*, can help reinforce your intentions and provide a concrete way for you to acknowledge the positive actions you are taking. Self-statements are one of the 12 tools taught in this workbook and play a key role in cementing the success of all of the tool sets to calm emotional flooding. You'll become far more familiar with the reasoning behind and regular use of self-statements in the upcoming chapters of this workbook. However, your use of them begins now.

The positive affirmations that you'll be guided to say to yourself at the end of your Daily Stress Inoculation are listed next. Once you've taken a few minutes to familiarize yourself with your closing affirmations, you'll be ready to follow along to the audio track and do your first run-through of the Daily Stress Inoculation.

I've taken time to take care of myself

I am taking action to lower my baseline stress temperature

I am taking action to increase the presence of protective neurochemicals

I maintain a habit of practicing the DSI

I open myself to relaxation, stillness, and calm

I carry this feeling of calm resilience with me throughout my day

Practicing the Daily Stress Inoculation

Now that you have learned the eye roll, tight fist, and focusing on the breath, created your safe place, and familiarized yourself with the closing affirmations, you're ready to sit back, relax, and enjoy trying out the Daily Stress Inoculation. Go to a quiet, comfortable place where you won't be disturbed and play Track 4 of the audio recording.

Just to recap, for the Daily Stress Inoculation you'll be progressing through the following five exercises:

- Eye Roll
- Tight Fist
- Focusing on the Breath
- Safe Place
- Closing Affirmations

GETTING INTO THE HABIT

"It takes 40 days to change a habit, 120 days to master the habit and a thousand days for the new habit to become who you are." —SHAKTA KAUR KHALSA

— **Selecting the right setting:** Just as with your time-out, it is important that the environment that you choose for your DSI is conducive to relaxation. Make sure the space you choose is one in which you can get comfortable, relax, and feel safe and secure. You might also wish to do a few things to embellish the *actual* physical environment in which you'll be engaging in this experience as well. Some people light a candle or burn incense. Others make sure a favorite pillow or throw blanket is present. Feel free to add any personal touches that might enhance your overall experience.

— **Do not disturb!** In the DSI, you are setting aside 15 minutes for yourself and only yourself. Think of it: in just 15 minutes a day you are creating a mini-sanctuary for yourself, where you create your own self-soothing emotional spa and engage in exercises that facilitate deep relaxation. We also suggest that you turn all phone ringers off for this 15 minute period of time. If you are doing your DSI at home when other family members are around, it is always a good idea to communicate that you are taking some time for yourself, and ask that you not be disturbed unless an emergency arises. Some even choose to put a "do not disturb" sign on the door to help remind any family members not to wander in while you're in the middle of your daily relaxation routine. Ideally, you should pick a time and place for your DSI in which you were less likely to be interrupted. For example, if you choose to do your DSI while on a break at work, make sure you can secure a place where you have privacy and are not likely to be disturbed.

— **Creating a ritual:** People are creatures of habit. The more you incorporate your practice of the DSI into a consistent, daily routine, the more likely you are to successfully engage this practice on a daily basis. For this reason it can be helpful to incorporate the DSI into a morning or evening ritual that you do as you are getting ready to begin the day or are gearing down for bed at the day's end. If you wish to incorporate your DSI into your regular workday, it can be helpful to have two consistent DSI rituals: one for workdays and one for weekends/days off. Remember: the more often and consistently you practice the DSI, the more likely you are to have success.

— **Setting reminders:** Whether it's a note taped to the bathroom mirror, an electronic notification on your phone or personal computer, or a daily alarm set to go off on your digital watch, visual or audio reminders can help you ensure that the DSI doesn't slip your mind. This is especially the case when you are just beginning to practice the DSI and have not had time to establish the DSI as a regular daily ritual. (An electronic notification tool also comes with this workbook's free companion app, The Road to Calm Companion App. We suggest downloading the app from the Google Play or Apple App Store and setting up your automated reminders now.)

— **Track your success:** When you're first starting out, keep a record of the days you've practiced the DSI (along with the days you've missed). This is a great way to see your successes on paper and gain a sense of accomplishment as you look at a completed checklist recording your efforts. It's also a useful tool if you're having trouble practicing the routine consistently. By checking off the days when you have successfully practiced, you may see some patterns cropping up that can help you identify possible common factors that influence your success in engaging in the practice. Conversely, you might identify common factors that contribute to your missing the daily practice and use this knowledge to help you avoid these pitfalls and enhance your success.

DAILY STRESS INOCULATION LOG

You can use the following log as you're starting the DSI practice to check off the days in which you've completed the exercise.

Week 1	Week 2	Week 3	Week 4
Day 1 ☐	Day 1 ☐	Day 1 ☐	Day 1 ☐
Day 2 ☐	Day 2 ☐	Day 2 ☐	Day 2 ☐
Day 3 ☐	Day 3 ☐	Day 3 ☐	Day 3 ☐
Day 4 ☐	Day 4 ☐	Day 4 ☐	Day 4 ☐
Day 5 ☐	Day 5 ☐	Day 5 ☐	Day 5 ☐
Day 6 ☐	Day 6 ☐	Day 6 ☐	Day 6 ☐
Day 7 ☐	Day 7 ☐	Day 7 ☐	Day 7 ☐

Take-Away Points

— Daily practice of the DSI lowers your baseline stress levels and lessens your susceptibility to emotional flooding.

— Strengthen your success with the following tips:

- Like they say in real estate, *location location location*. Select a setting for your DSI that is conducive to rest and relaxation.
- Choose a time and place where you're not likely to be disturbed.
- Incorporate the DSI into part of a daily ritual.
- Use The Road to Calm Companion App, sticky notes, or other electronic devices to set reminders for yourself to help ensure the DSI doesn't slip your mind—especially when you're first starting to make it a habit.

— Use the checklist provided in this workbook to track your success!

Mastering Basic Calming Actions: The STOP Solution ("S", "T", "O")

THE STOP SOLUTION IS A CLEAR, CONCRETE, AND SIMPLE COURSE OF ACTION that can transform your experience of emotional flooding, issuing a cease-fire to the midbrain gone rogue.

The STOP Solution

S Scan for thoughts, emotions, behaviors, and sensations in your body that indicate emotional flooding is either occurring or on its way.

T Take a time-out.

O Overcome Initial Flooding using the fast-acting interventions to de-escalate runaway emotions.

P Put the 12 tools into practice.

After reading this chapter, you will have mastered S T O—Scan, Take a time-out, and Overcome Initial Flooding. In Chapter 6 you will learn the 12 Tools, and then in Chapters 7 and 8, you will learn the "P"—Putting the tools into practice. It is essential that you master the first three self-soothing skills before learning the final part of the STOP Solution—the specific affect-regulation tools you need, based on the particular stressor you are facing. The calming actions you take in these first three steps are quick, easy to implement, and will *always* precede your application of the tools (see Figure 5.1).

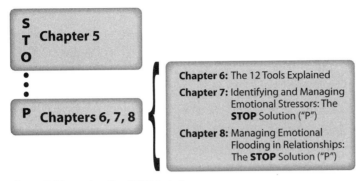

Figure 5.1 Learning the **STOP** Solution

Scan for Thoughts, Emotions, Behaviors, and Sensations

 Even flash floods have warning signs: the darkening of the skies as storm clouds set in over the horizon; distant rumblings of thunder; the gathering sound of a rush of incoming tides. No matter how quickly and how powerfully floods strike, there are signs of their imminent arrival. This is also the case with emotional flooding. Given the sudden intensity with which emotional flooding strikes, it is easy to overlook what's happening until you're in the midst of a torrent of emotion. But there are precursors. Rather than being swept away in the flood of your own emotions, the first step is getting in the habit of scanning your thoughts, emotions, behaviors, and sensations, even when things are going smoothly. In this way you will learn to recognize the presence of emotional flooding, which gives you the opportunity to spring into action with the calming techniques you will learn in the remainder of this workbook.

TIPS FOR SCANNING

— Become familiar with your own flooding profile (see later).

— Throughout each day, even when things are going smoothly, pause several times to scan your thoughts, emotions, behaviors, and sensations.

— Especially when you recognize that you are beginning to get upset, be sure to follow the scanning procedure.

CREATING YOUR FLOODING PROFILE

The following sections will help you recognize and understand your unique flooding profile. Make sure you have a pen or pencil, as you will be compiling a list of your own markers of emotional flooding for each of the four categories of indicators: Thoughts, Emotions (Affect), Behaviors, and Physical Sensations.

Thoughts

Your thoughts reflect your experience of the present and past, and shape your expectations of the future. They also reflect the way you are interpreting incoming information from your external *and* internal environment. Being mindful of your thoughts, therefore, can help alert you when your system is gearing up for an overreaction—or that the overreaction is already in full swing. The following list is composed of thoughts that often accompany emotional flooding. Circle any that apply to you. There is also space for you to add any other thoughts that belong on your flooding profile.

— *I can't take this anymore.*
— *This is a disaster.*
— *I can't face this.*
— *I should have never left the house this morning.*
— *I'm trapped.*
— *I'll never survive this.*
— *This is not going to end well.*
— *I* have *to have that* _____ *[food/drink/thing/activity].*
— *This is too much for me to handle.*
— *I want to scream.*
— *There's no way I can get this all done.*
— *I'm losing control.*
— *I wish I could hit something right now.*
— *I really want to grab him/her and shake him/her.*
— *I feel helpless.*
— *I feel weak.*
— *If anyone says the wrong thing to me today, they're going to wish they hadn't.*

— *Please don't let anything go wrong today, because I can't handle it.*

— *My heart's about to beat right out of my chest!*

_____

_____

_____

Emotions

Emotions are feeling-rich experiences that can vary in degrees of intensity. They are transitory, meaning that if you wait long enough, they will pass. Yet a powerful, painful emotion can seem to last an eternity even if it does indeed pass in only a few minutes' time. Emotions can also belie logic or reason. Just because you tell yourself you should be feeling a certain way does not mean that your emotions will follow suit. Further belying logic or reason, you can also experience multiple, seemingly contradictory emotions simultaneously. An experience that you think should elicit happiness and contentment might bring up a combination of happiness, frustration, and agitation. Thus, rather than trying to control or dictate your emotions, it is far more beneficial to *observe* and *respond* to your ever-changing emotional states.

Keen observation begins with awareness of what to be on the lookout for. The following list is composed of thoughts that accompany emotional flooding. Circle any that apply to you. There are also empty spaces for you to add any common combinations of emotions and thoughts that belong on your flooding profile.

— Fear	— Anger	— Grief
— Terror	— Rage	— Sorrow
— Panic	— Outrage	— Despair
— Nervousness	— Hate	— Hopelessness
— Apprehension	— Frustration	— Helplessness
— Trepidation	— Aggravation	— Shame
— Concern	— Resentment	— Dread
— Worry	— Impatience	— Inadequacy
— Disquiet	— Irritability	— Failure
— Alarm	— Sadness	— Exhaustion

_____

_____

_____

Behaviors

Behaviors bring action to your thoughts, emotions, and sensations. For example, if you are upset, you might begin to bite your nails or fidget with your car keys; if you are feeling irritable, you might speak sharply to your coworker; if your heart starts racing, you might stop your work and do an internet search for possible causes, focusing all your attention on this new distressing sensation.

The following list is composed of behaviors that often accompany emotional flooding. Circle any that apply to you. There are also empty spaces for you to add more concrete descriptions of the behaviors that go hand in hand with your experiences of emotional flooding. You might, for example, elaborate on a particular way you instigate or escalate conflicts, or particular ways that you isolate. If you find you need more space, don't hesitate to grab a separate sheet of paper.

— Snapping at friends/family/ coworkers/strangers
— Instigating an argument
— Escalating a conflict
— Overeating
— Drinking excessively
— Engaging in repetitive movement or action (e.g., biting nails, fiddling with an object)
— Difficulty sitting still
— Using recreational drugs excessively

— Impulse buying
— Acting or speaking before thinking
— Engaging in risky sexual behavior
— Withdrawing from others
— Isolating
— Clenching your jaw or tightening your shoulders

_____

_____

_____

Physical Sensations

When you experience a strong emotion or even a thought influenced by emotion, there are accompanying reactions in your body. However, like many people, you may be unaware of your body's signals and ignore this valuable resource that reflects your emotional states. Or if you are prone to anxiety, you might be very aware of your bodily sensations but overreact to the sensations and misinterpret their meaning.

The following is a list of physical sensations that often accompany emotional flooding. Circle any that are familiar to you. There are also empty spaces for you to add other sensations that go hand in hand with your experiences of emotional flooding.

— Lightheadedness	— Cold sweats
— Dizziness	— Tingling in hands or feet
— A sensation of shakiness	— Cold/clammy hands or feet
— Racing/pounding heartbeat	— Muscle weakness
— Nausea	— Muscle tension/tightness
— Stomach pains/cramping	— Fatigue and exhaustion
— Butterflies in your stomach	— Labored movements
— Stomach upsets	— Trouble getting out of bed in the
— Hot flashes	morning

_____

_____

_____

The fight-or-flight response can be triggered by any of the thoughts, emotions, behaviors, and sensations you identified. As you learned in Chapter 4, when you sense a possible threat to your safety or well-being, the sympathetic nervous system (SNS) kicks in. The SNS floods your body with the fuel it needs (for example, chemical messengers such as adrenaline and norepinephrine) to respond instantaneously to a threat and protect you from harm. It is the SNS that mobilizes you to either fight or flee. So, many of the physical sensations associated with the intense anger or fear that can occur during emotional flooding are the result of the SNS at work. For example, when revved, the SNS diverts blood flow to major muscle groups that would aid you in successfully fighting or running. When you're flooded with anger, the surge of energy you feel and the increased desire to use your arms or legs to express this anger is due to the SNS's mobilization. The revving SNS also increases the supply of oxygen to the parts of your body that will aid your defense. This is why breathing and heart rate often quicken with the activation of the fight-or-flight response. Yet these physical sensations can fuel panic when you're flooded with anxiety. For example, the fear that the markers of SNS activation indicate a heart attack or other health crisis often worsens the flooding and increases emotional distress.

This is why, in developing your own flooding profile, it is important to understand the workings of the fight-or-flight response, as many of the physical sensations you experience during anger- and anxiety-related emotional flooding (i.e., many of the bullet points that follow) are either directly or indirectly related to SNS arousal.

The parasympathetic nervous system (PNS), on the other hand, acts as the brakes to the SNS, slowing and calming your body to counteract the revving of the SNS. When working optimally together, the two systems give you the ability to rev up in response to danger and then slow down when the threat is gone. When emotional flooding occurs, however, the parasympathetic nervous system often fails to kick in, leaving the SNS to continue to rev up when you really want it to be revving down. The STOP Solution teaches you to engage the PNS. So by learning and engaging the tools, you are literally learning to calm emotional flooding by putting the brakes on in your nervous system.

The SNS does not play a key role in all types of emotional flooding. Sadness, hopelessness, and despair create a type of emotional flooding that in the absence of concurrent anxiety or anger does not typically kick the SNS into action. Nevertheless, you still need to calm yourself. When you experience these types of emotional flooding, it is still important to engage the PNS. Doing so brings you into equilibrium, enabling you access to the logical forebrain, so that you can experience your emotions with perspective.

Whether the emotional flooding is fear, anger, sadness, or another emotion, it is a good habit to identify the bodily reactions that accompany these emotions. These physical sensations serve as warning signs that emotional flooding is imminent. In this way, you can begin to intervene with the tools to engage the parasympathetic nervous system before the reaction gets too far out of control.

T: Take a Time-Out When You Are Emotionally Flooded In Order To Calm and Center Yourself

After you have scanned your thoughts, emotions, behaviors, and physical sensations and recognized that you are in a reactive mode, the next part of the STOP Solution is to take a time-out. Time-outs are not just for children. The basic premise behind all the interventions in this workbook is that you can't just snap your fingers and turn off emotional flooding. When emotions are high, you need to stop the action and take a time-out. It is unrealistic to expect to reduce knee-jerk emotional reactions without taking a break to soothe the agitated nervous system and calm the mind. A break allows sufficient time to gain perspective and reevaluate your responses.

To effectively initiate time-outs, it is also essential that you have a clear plan of action. You don't want to begin planning your evacuation route when the floodwaters are already rushing your way. Likewise, preparation for your time-outs can aid their implementation. The following tips and guidelines can help you lay the groundwork for this success.

CRITERIA FOR SELECTING A PLACE FOR A TIME-OUT

— Private, where you will not be interrupted
— Comfortable, calming, and quiet (If you are in a public place, you can always go to the restroom to have some time alone.)

EXCUSING YOURSELF TO STOP FOR A TIME-OUT

— *When with significant others, close friends, and family*: We encourage you to share the STOP procedure with family and close friends in advance so they understand when you excuse yourself to take a time-out.
— *When with coworkers or acquaintances*: Excusing yourself to go to a restroom is a socially acceptable way to leave your current location quickly without explanation. The alternative is to explain that you need to take a break for a moment and then find a private location.

If you can't find a getaway for your time-out, you can still use the following techniques to calm your emotions.

O: Overcome Initial Flooding

"Quiet the mind and the soul will speak."　　　　—MA JAYA SATI BHAGAVATI, **YOGA TEACHER**

Once you've settled into the space you've chosen for your time-out, and even if you are unable to get away for privacy, this part of the STOP Solution—Overcome Initial Flooding—allows you to quickly interrupt imminent or full emotional flooding.

You've already learned and have been practicing the Eye Roll, Tight Fist, and Focusing on the Breath in your Daily Stress Inoculation. You will also use these quick-calming techniques to Overcome Initial Flooding during your time-out. These three techniques serve to swiftly dial down heightened emotions and are effective whenever you use the STOP Solution.

For your convenience, we have repeated the directions for each of these techniques.

DIRECTIONS FOR EYE ROLL

1. Roll your eyes upward as if you were trying to look at the centermost point in the arch of each of your eyebrows.
2. As you roll your eyes upward, take in a slow, deep breath.
3. Hold your eyes upward while holding your breath for a few seconds.
4. Exhale slowly and lower your eyes to their original position.

DIRECTIONS FOR TIGHT FIST

1. Imagine all your worry, fear, and muscular tension going into your dominant hand.
2. Make a fist with that hand, squeeze it tightly, and feel the tension.
3. Magnify it and tighten that fist even more.
4. Imagine that tension becoming a liquid of any color you choose; the liquid represents your distress, worry, and discomfort in your body.
5. Gradually release your fist and imagine the colored liquid flowing to the floor and through the floor to the ground, to be absorbed deep into the soil.

6. You can repeat squeezing your fist and releasing the liquid again, noticing the difference between tension and relaxation.

7. Repeat the exercise with your other hand.

DIRECTIONS FOR FOCUSING ON THE BREATH

1. Observe your breathing without trying to change it.

2. Spend some time noticing the temperature, rhythm, and pace of your breath.

3. Think the word "comfort" as you inhale and "relax" as you exhale.

4. Experience a sensation of floating and the relief that comes from attending to the breath.

STOP for Mini Time-Outs

PURPOSE

— To establish an ongoing resilience to stress

— To reset the nervous system and elicit the calm state achieved in the DSI

— To reinforce the habit of taking a time-out

Mini time-outs are preventative medicine because, with practice, you develop the skill of returning to calm throughout the day. By re-eliciting the state of equilibrium that you achieve in the DSI by taking *mini time-outs* 3–5 times throughout the day, you are countering the natural accumulation of stress that all of us experience in our daily lives. In mini time-outs, you engage the three Overcome Initial Flooding tools, followed by an affirmative self-statement. It can feel very satisfying to give yourself a couple of minutes a few times a day to push the refresh button and receive a bit of calm. Additionally, weaving mini time-outs into your schedule creates a very important habit. Then, when emotional flooding inevitably arises, you are more likely to STOP and initiate a needed time-out. The more you practice the quick, calming tools, the more powerful they become, so mini time-outs also enhance the effectiveness of the time-outs you do take. This gives you more control over emotional flooding when it does arise.

DIRECTIONS FOR MINI TIME-OUTS

1. Listen to audio track 2 or perform The Eye Roll, Tight Fist, and Focusing on the Breath from memory.

2. Close your mini time-outs with an affirming self-statement. For example: "I am in control of my reactions" or "I honor myself by making time to take mini time-outs."

Creating Opportunities for Mini Time-Outs

There are two approaches to taking mini time-outs. The first is to establish set times or circumstances for practicing them. The second is to fit in your mini time-outs during routine or unexpected free moments. Following are some suggestions for when to take mini time-outs:

— when booting up your computer
— at lunch or a coffee break
— before brushing your teeth
— before you enter your office in the morning or your house after work
— when you are on hold on the phone

Use the following chart to list four times each day when you plan to STOP for mini time-outs.

SCHEDULE FOR MINI TIME-OUTS

1. _____
2. _____
3. _____
4. _____

Take-Away Points

— Use your flooding profile to help you STOP and scan your Thoughts, Emotions, Behaviors, and Sensations that indicate an overreaction is on the way.

— Quickly STOP to engage in time-outs when needed.

— Let people you're close to know that you will STOP for a time-out as needed.

- Have the audio tracks and companion app that accompany this workbook handy to use whenever you STOP.
- Decide on private, comfortable locations at home and work where you can STOP for a time-out.
- The key is to STOP and take a time-out *whenever* it's needed. Although it is easier to take a time-out at a time or place where you have privacy in a quiet setting, if necessary you can take a time-out even when you're around other people or in a less-than-ideal environment.

The 12 Tools Explained

 THIS CHAPTER PRESENTS THE 12 TOOLS TO CALM RUNAWAY EMOTIONS THAT you will use in various combinations when you STOP for your time-outs. Whether you use all 12 tools on a regular basis or not, it is helpful to familiarize yourself with all of them—especially because you will be using various combinations of the tools during your time-outs to effectively calm the type of emotional flooding you are currently experiencing. In this chapter the purpose of and directions for each tool are described, and an audio track allows you to try out each exercise. If there are occasions when you would prefer to use the tools from memory during your time-outs rather than play the audio recordings, the step-by-step instructions presented in this chapter can also provide a quick reference point to jog your memory. Finally, the Reflections section after each tool gives you space to journal any thoughts or notes regarding your use of each tool.

The 12 Tools

1. **MINDFULNESS WITH DETACHED OBSERVATION**
   (audio track 5)

2. **OKAY SIGNAL**
   (audio tracks 6 and 7)

3. **DIALING DOWN REACTIVITY**
   (audio track 8)

4. **HEAVY HANDS, HEAVY LEGS**
   (audio track 9)

5. IMAGINARY SUPPORT CIRCLE
   (audio track 10)

6. WISE SELF
   (audio track 11)

7. EMPATHIC SELF
   (audio track 12)

8. REMEMBERING SUCCESSES
   (audio track 13)

9. POSITIVE FUTURE-FOCUSING
   (audio track 14)

10. JUXTAPOSITION OF TWO THOUGHTS/FEELINGS
    (audio track 15)

11. POSTPONEMENT
    (audio track 16)

12. SELF-STATEMENTS
    (audio track 17)

TOOL 1: MINDFULNESS WITH DETACHED OBSERVATION

PURPOSE
— Focus awareness on the present moment.
— Eliminate self-criticism and judgment when negative thoughts or feelings emerge.
— Replace judgment with curiosity.

Mindfulness is the practice of calm, detached observation of your current experience. It is about focusing attention on the moment, simply observing with curiosity each thought, feeling, or sensation as it comes, goes, and is replaced by another and yet another. Unlike traditional mindfulness meditation, you will be using mindfulness to create calm in order to gain new perspective on charged situations.

It is a truism that thoughts, feelings, and sensations are like busses: If you wait a few minutes, another one will be along shortly. With mindfulness, the goal is not to change the emotions, sensations, or thoughts that you are experiencing, but rather to accept them and acknowledge their transient nature and to be accepting and open to what is.

Another key component of mindfulness is a lack of self-judgment. This is at the essence of "detached observation." You may be familiar with that internal voice that narrates your present experience, evaluating the ongoing chain of events by making value judgments. When you notice that your heart is beginning to race or your anger is increasing, that voice of judgment might chime in with something along the lines of "oh no…" or "I shouldn't be thinking this." When practicing mindfulness with detached observation, you start replacing knee-jerk thoughts of "this is good" or "this is bad/horrible/not okay" with "this is present/happening." You replace judgment with curiosity, taking a step back to simply observe your experience. You might observe, "There's the worried thought" or "Hmm, there is an angry feeling." This stance of detached observation serves to decrease your reactivity to the thoughts, feelings, and sensations you experience. By using the tool of mindfulness with detached observation, you are changing the lens through which you view your experience and, in doing so, you may find that the experience changes.

DIRECTIONS

1. Observe thoughts, feelings, or sensations.
2. Name the thoughts, feelings, or sensations (e.g., "I observe the frustration)."
3. Take an attitude of curiosity about your experience (e.g., "As I observe how frustrated I am, I notice my jaw clenching)."
4. Remind yourself that thoughts, feelings, and sensations come and go.
5. Now that you are no longer flooded with emotion, ask yourself *if* you want to respond to the trigger that prompted this.

Listen to the recording for audio track 5.

(Adapted with permission from W. W. Norton & Company, Inc.

Copyright © 2007 by Carolyn Daitch.)

Reflections

What was it like to sit and observe your experience? What emotions, physical sensations, and running commentary in your mind emerged? Did you notice any judgment cropping up—judgment of your thoughts, sensations, or emotions?

_____

_____

_____

_____

_____

Were you able to step back, detach, and be a curious observer of your present experience? If so, what was that like for you?

_____

_____

_____

_____

_____

_____

Can you think of different scenarios in the future where you can use this tool?

_____

_____

_____

_____

_____

_____

TOOL 2: OKAY SIGNAL

PURPOSE

— Elicit a sense of calm and well-being quickly.

— Associate that positive state with a hand signal or cue (an okay signal).

— Remember that you can only live in the present moment and that in the present moment everything is okay.

— Use the okay signal as a quick reset button for the nervous system to re-elicit this sense of well-being.

Across many cultures the okay signal is used as a common, universal hand gesture to indicate that everything is okay. As the diagram indicates, you create this gesture by placing the tips of your thumb and forefinger together to form a circle. While this gesture is usually used to communicate with others, in this exercise you will be using this hand signal to communicate a message of well-being to yourself. To do this, you will be using the okay signal to create what we call a *sensory cue*.

A sensory cue is used to elicit, or cue, a desired emotional state. The brain is adept at linking emotional states with sensory cues. One powerful example of sensory cueing that most people are familiar with occurs with the sense of smell. How many times have you walked into a friend's kitchen or a restaurant and taken in a smell that brings you right back to a moment in your childhood? Maybe the smell brought you back to your grandmother's kitchen as she lifted a tin of hot blueberry muffins out of the oven. And as the sensory cue in the present elicits the memory of the past, feelings associated with the initial experience—in this case feelings of warmth and contentment—arise.

While smells provide powerful sensory cues, hand gestures are far more practical for everyday use. As such, when you engage in the okay signal exercise you can generate a state of well-being and then be guided through steps to link the okay signal to a positive emotional experience.

Like the creation of your safe place(s) for the Daily Stress Inoculation in Chapter 4, you will first create the sensory cue of the okay signal using audio track 6. Once this sensory cue is created you needn't revisit this track. Rather, you will use audio track 7 during your time-outs to activate the "okay" sensory cue and re-elicit the associated state of well-being. This is a powerful way to interrupt emotional flooding and cue an altogether different state of being in which you strongly connect to the feeling that everything really is, indeed, okay.

DIRECTIONS FOR LEARNING THE OKAY SIGNAL

1. Elicit a state of calm, where you are relaxed, at ease, and have a sense of well-being.

2. With one hand, make an "okay signal" (pressing the thumb and forefinger together to make a circle).

3. Still holding the okay signal, repeat to yourself three times "I am okay in this moment."

4. Imagine using this okay signal as a cue in difficult situations to re-elicit this feeling of peaceful well-being when you are feeling flooded.

Listen to the recording for audio track 6.

DIRECTIONS FOR IMPLEMENTING THE OKAY SIGNAL

1. Remind yourself that you have the ability to use your okay signal to cue a sense of calm and feelings of well-being.

2. Make the okay signal with one of your hands, accompanied by phrases such as "Everything is okay in this moment."

3. Notice as emotional overwhelm is replaced by the sense of well-being that the okay signal cues.

Listen to the recording for audio track 7.

Reflections

How did you feel after you put your thumb and forefinger together, associating it with a state of well-being?

_____

_____

_____

_____

_____

_____

_____

How did you feel when you added phrases such as "everything is okay in this moment . . . I am okay in this moment . . . I can handle what is happening in this moment"?

_____

_____

_____

_____

_____

_____

_____

Describe different scenarios in the future when you can use this tool.

_____

_____

_____

_____

_____

_____

TOOL 3: DIALING DOWN REACTIVITY

PURPOSE

— Determine your ideal level of emotional reactivity in response to a trigger you are experiencing.

— Acknowledge the discrepancy between your current level of emotional reactivity and your ideal level of reaction.

— Visualize an image that will help you "dial down" and calibrate your current level of emotional activation.

It would be nice if you could regulate the intensity of your emotions much in the same way you can regulate the temperature on an oven when you are cooking. If you want to turn the temperature up, just turn the dial to the desired setting and the temperature gradually starts to rise until it reaches the desired degree. A little too hot? Just shift the dial a few degrees to the left, and the temperature immediately starts to cool down. And when you're done cooking, you just ease the dial to the "off" position and the temperature will immediately begin its cooling descent, degree by degree, back to room temperature.

The dialing down reactivity tool teaches you to visualize a dial to recalibrate the intensity of emotion you are experiencing. Now let's say your emotions are running way too hot, say at the level of 9 on a scale of 1 to 10. Using the tool of this dial, you can dial down the intensity of the heat of emotion to your desired level. Let's say a 3. Using this tool of a dial, you can learn to "dial down" the intensity of the emotion so that you control the intensity of your emotions.

DIRECTIONS

1. Visualize a dial that registers your degree of emotional flooding, with values ranging from 1 to 10.
2. Visualize the dial registering the amount of emotional flooding you are currently experiencing.
3. Access a part of yourself that can view your current challenge with a sense of proportion and perspective. Now ask yourself what the ideal level of emotional reactivity should be—the level that is congruent with what is needed to respond to the situation you are currently facing.
4. Visualize the dial slowly lowering and, as it lowers, so does your level of emotional distress.
5. Notice the newfound sense of empowerment that comes with the ability to "dial down" your emotional reactivity whenever you wish.

Listen to the recording for audio track 8.

Reflections

What does the dial you created look like? What color is the background? What color is the needle? What color are the numbers? Where is your dial: on a wall, on a desk, or floating in midair?

_____

_____

_____

_____

_____

_____

When you were practicing the exercise what number did your dial initially register? What is your ideal range that you would like your dial to stay in?

_____

_____

_____

_____

_____

_____

_____

Did you notice any changes in how your body feels as you dialed down your reactivity, and if so, how? Describe how your thoughts settled down or changed, and if so, how? How did your emotions change?

_____

_____

_____

_____

_____

_____

_____

Describe different scenarios in the future where you can use this tool.

_____

_____

_____

_____

_____

_____

_____

TOOL 4: HEAVY HANDS, HEAVY LEGS

PURPOSE

— Counter physiological agitation with muscle relaxation

— Release muscle tension with sensations of limb heaviness

— Associate the sensation of limb heaviness with relaxation and calm

— Link physical relaxation with calming self-statements

Just as the physical sensations of a racing heartbeat or shakiness in the limbs are often associated with states of emotional agitation, there are also physical sensations that are associated with states of relaxation. The feeling of arm and leg heaviness is one such sensation. It is a phenomenon that people often report experiencing when in deep states of relaxation. Tool #4 is one component of a stress reduction approach called autogenics, which was developed by Johannes Schultz, a German psychiatrist and neurologist who found that the relaxation response is characteristically accompanied by certain physical sensations.

The ability to generate the sensation of heaviness at will is a great tool to have in your arsenal to diffuse emotional flooding and heightened reactivity. Earlier we discussed how physical sensations accompany emotional flooding. Heavy Hands, Heavy Legs is a tool that counters this physiological reactivity, using your own physiology to quickly and powerfully create states of relaxation and calm.

DIRECTIONS

1. Focus on your right hand and repeat six times, "My right hand is getting heavy."

2. Focus on your left hand and repeat six times, "My left hand is getting heavy."

3. Imagine that there are lead weights on your wrists, making your hands very heavy, and feel the heaviness (and the relaxation that accompanies it) spreading up to your arms.

4. As you continue to notice the feelings of heaviness and relaxation, repeat six times, "My arms are heavy, and I am feeling safe and calm."

5. Now allow the heaviness to spread to your legs. Focus on your right leg and repeat six times, "My right leg is getting heavy."

6. Focus on your left leg and repeat six times, "My left leg is getting heavy."

7. Notice the heaviness in your arms and legs and the relaxation that this brings about. Finally, as you continue to notice the feelings of heaviness and relaxation, repeat six times, "My arms and legs are heavy, and I am feeling safe and calm."

Listen to the recording for audio track 9.

Reflections

How did you experience heaviness in your hands? In your legs? What sensations arose? Did you notice a pleasant relaxation that accompanied the heaviness? What other sensations, if any, did you experience, such as warmth? Were you able to experience other sensations of relaxation and ease that accompanied the heaviness?

_____

_____

_____

_____

_____

_____

_____

What, if any, visual prompts did you use to promote this feeling?

_____

_____

_____

_____

_____

_____

_____

What are some different scenarios in the future where you can use this tool?

_____

_____

_____

_____

_____

_____

TOOL 5: IMAGINARY SUPPORT CIRCLE

PURPOSE

— Envision a network of real or imagined people or entities who care for your personal well-being.

— Experience feelings of connection and support.

— Acknowledge that you have resources.

The instinct to seek comfort, nurturance, and emotional support from others is part and parcel to the human condition. The desire to experience connection with others is, in fact, one of the reasons that interpersonal conflict can be the cause of such great distress—including emotional flooding. When your attempts at connection fail in the moment, you are denied the sense of well-being that you are seeking through shared connection and relationship. When you experience overwhelming emotion, the ability to generate feelings of safety, comfort, and support associated with interpersonal connection can be crucial to regaining a sense of emotional equilibrium and dampening emotional flooding. This is especially the case when the emotional flooding occurs in response to interpersonal conflict or an interpersonal stressor.

The imaginary support circle allows you to harness the immensely powerful resource of interpersonal connection during times when you are emotionally flooded. Your nervous systems are hard-wired in such a way that the care, support, and emotional nurturance of others can be innately calming, soothing, and sustaining. Luckily, the immediate physical presence of a supportive person is not necessary to "turn on" key components of the neural circuitry activated by a sense of emotional connection. By creating and then accessing the imaginary support circle, you activate this neural circuitry.

With the imaginary support circle, you will assemble a group of caring figures whose imagined presence brings you a sense of well-being, connection, and support. These characters can be real or fictional, human or animal, living or long deceased. There's also no limit to the number of individuals you can include in your support circle, and the particular individuals you might call on to support you in any given instance can shift given your need on a particular day. What remains consistent is that this tool allows you to generate a palpable experience of emotional support that will eliminate the feeling of being alone. This perception fosters emotional equilibrium and calms emotional flooding.

DIRECTIONS

1. Recognize that you can create an imaginary circle of support that you can call upon at any time you feel alone or unsupported.

2. Close your eyes and create this circle of support as you, one by one, invite people/spiritual entities/animals in. (The people in your support circle can range from close friends or relatives to teachers, mentors, or even public figures or leaders whom you have never personally met. The support circle can also include religious or spiritual figures whom you find comforting. It can also include people or animals who have already passed away, but whose memory and presence comfort you.)

3. Look around your circle; look at the people you have invited in; and feel the support, wisdom, strength, and peaceful energy that each person brings to your circle.

4. Notice as emotional overwhelm is replaced by the sense of well-being that connection to your imaginary support circle brings.

Listen to the recording for audio track 10.

Reflections

Whom did you invite into your circle of support?

_____

_____

_____

_____

What are the desirable attributes each person/spiritual entity/presence/animal brings to your support circle?

_____

_____

_____

_____

In what different situations might you use this tool?

_____

_____

_____

_____

TOOL 6: WISE SELF

PURPOSE

— Imagine that you have created a part of yourself that is mature, wise, and disciplined.

— Invite this part of yourself to influence your perspective, your choices, and actions.

— Call on this aspect of yourself to help modulate your reactions to a situation that is creating emotional flooding.

You may sometimes notice that different people bring out different aspects of your personality. All of these are real parts of who you are. You can be playful, serious, spontaneous, task-oriented, disciplined, wistful, self-conscious, grounded, competent, wise, and empathic. The Tools 6 and

7 draw on these different parts that can serve as a resource for you when needed. In essence, you learn to call forth a part of yourself that is taking a backseat when you are emotionally flooded.

For Tool 6, the part of self that you access can be thought of as a *wise self*. It's the part of yourself that is grounded, wise, and mature. This is the part of you that should guide your reactions and behaviors. Yet, when you're flooded with emotion, the wise self is usually dormant. The overwhelm inherent in emotional flooding often brings to the forefront parts of the self that are less flexible, less disciplined, and less mature. During emotional flooding, it is easy to forget that the wise part even exists or is accessible to you. The following exercise teaches you how to call upon the wise self whenever it's needed.

DIRECTIONS

1. Recall a specific instance in which you felt wise, compassionate, disciplined, and mature.
2. Identify the part of yourself that is mature, compassionate, and wise. This part of yourself helps you act with awareness of your own and others' needs, in ways that are congruent with your core values.
3. Bring awareness and attention to what it feels like when you have engaged this part of yourself, and it is guiding your reactions and decisions.
4. Recognize that you can access this mature part of yourself whenever you are in need of a wise and compassionate inner parent to help inform your actions and help you respond to any challenges you are experiencing.

Listen to the recording for audio track 11.

Reflections

Describe a specific instance in which you felt wise, compassionate, disciplined, and mature. Could you connect to a kind yet firm and disciplined inner parent? If so, remember the details of that experience. Where were you? What was the context of the situation?

_____

_____

_____

_____

Describe how accessing this part can help you manage your emotional flooding.

_____

_____

_____

_____

In what specific situations in the future might you use this tool?

_____

_____

_____

_____

TOOL 7: EMPATHIC SELF

PURPOSE

— Imagine that you have a part of yourself that is compassionate, nurturing, and empathic toward yourself and others.

— Invite this part of yourself to shape your perspective, choices, and actions toward yourself and others.

— Call on this part of yourself to help modulate overreactions.

This tool teaches you to call forth a part of yourself that is highly compassionate and empathic. This part of self is most easily accessed when you're caring for a child or supporting a friend or loved one during a difficult time. However, the empathic, compassionate part of self is usually far from the scene when you are in the midst of a conflict and feel angry, frustrated, disappointed, or hurt. It is also distant when you're frustrated with yourself and feeling a flood of self-recrimination. When you are flooded by emotions such as anger or self-criticism, it is crucial to call on the compassionate and empathic part of yourself. The following exercise provides you with the skills to make this a reality.

DIRECTIONS

1. Acknowledge that you have many different parts of your personality that you can access.

2. Identify the specific part of yourself that is empathic, compassionate, caring, and nurturing.

3. Recall a specific instance in which you felt empathic, compassionate, and nurturing.

4. Bring awareness and attention to what it feels like when you have engaged this part of yourself, and it is guiding your reactions and decisions.

5. Recognize that you can access this part of yourself whenever you need empathy to guide your reactions and responses to yourself and to others and to help you respond to strong feelings of judgment, anger, or intolerance.

Listen to the recording for audio track 12.

Reflections

In what specific instances have you connected with another person with empathy, compassion, support, and care? Describe the details of that experience. Where were you? For whom did you feel empathy? What was the context of the interaction?

_____

_____

_____

_____

_____

How was this experience enriching, fulfilling, or heartwarming for you?

_____
_____
_____
_____
_____

In what different scenarios in the future do you anticipate using this tool?

_____
_____
_____
_____
_____

TOOL 8: REMEMBERING SUCCESSES

"Don't cry because it's over, smile because it happened." —DR. SEUSS

PURPOSE

— Remind yourself that you have successfully coped with and overcome challenges in the past.

— Reexperience past feelings of mastery and success in the present moment.

— Harness the strength of those successes and use them to empower you in the present and future.

When you're flooded with intense emotion, it's easy to forget your strengths and capabilities and believe that you are unable to meet the challenge you are facing. When feeling overwhelmed, you perceive that your strengths are not sufficient to meet the challenge you're currently facing. This may be reinforced by previous difficulties quelling overwhelming emotions. You and others may have tried to talk you out of overreactivity and failed because logic-based strategies may not be sufficient to lessen reactivity.

Empowerment is the antidote to being overwhelmed. With the 12 tools you are giving yourself the power to turn the tide. With Tool 8, you harness the strength and empowerment gained from previous experiences of success to empower you now, when you are emotionally flooded. Remembering Successes, which you will learn with the following audio track, teaches you to dissipate emotional flooding.

DIRECTIONS

1. Recall the times when you have met a challenge and have coped with it successfully.

2. Focus your attention on the feelings you had during these instances of success and bring these feelings into the present moment. Try smiling to yourself as you do so.

3. Remember the physical sensations and posture that accompanied these experiences of success. You might experiment with trying on the same posture now.

4. Allow these feelings of success and the experience of your capabilities to bolster your confidence and resilience when you confront present and future challenges.

Listen to the recording for audio track 13.

Reflections

Describe in as much detail as possible some of your experiences of successfully overcoming challenges. What feelings accompanied these positive memories?

_____

_____

_____

_____

_____

How do these memories of past successes and the accompanying feelings bolster your sense of ability in the present?

_____

_____

_____

_____

_____

In what scenarios in the future do you anticipate using this tool?

_____

_____

_____

_____

TOOL 9: POSITIVE FUTURE-FOCUSING

PURPOSE

— Remind yourself that in the future your consistent use of the tools will enable you to quickly reestablish emotional equilibrium.

— Use this knowledge to enhance your sense of well-being in the present.

"It is a peculiarity of man that he can only live by looking to the future." —VIKTOR FRANKL

When you experience emotional flooding, the surge of emotion can trick your mind and body into feeling as if your very survival is at stake, even though this is not usually the case. This is especially true when the emotions consist of fear or anger. With Tool 9, Positive Future-Focusing, you purposefully shift your attention *away from* the present moment and fast-forward, in your mind's eye, to the near future when the sense of danger has receded. You might even fast-forward to the moment when you're in a completely different scene. By changing the envisioned scenario, you change the way your body and mind respond. Envisioning the experience of safety and relief cues your body and mind to shift away from the survival-based, reactive mode that feeds emotional flooding.

Positive Future-Focusing provides you with another means of cueing the parasympathetic nervous system (as do the Daily Stress Inoculation and the Overcome Initial Flooding tools in the time-out) to put on the brakes when your emotions are revving out of control. You invoke and experience

The 12 Tools Explained

the safety, security, and sense of well-being that comes with knowing, in every cell of your body, that you are out of the danger zone.

DIRECTIONS

1. Acknowledge that you are capable of bringing about changes in yourself and your life.

2. Recognize that you have the ability to "fast-forward" in your imagination to a time when the challenge that currently feels overwhelming has resolved and the emotional discomfort has subsided.

3. Imagine a future time when you will feel better or the stressor has been resolved. Depending on your trigger, this future time may be in the near or more distant future. If the troubling scenario is something that's not going to change, you might imagine a time in the future when your coping mechanisms have developed so that you can diminish emotional flooding and reestablish emotional equilibrium quickly.

4. Allow yourself to feel satisfaction as you see yourself in the future with new behaviors, new qualities, and new ways of reacting or not reacting.

5. Tap into and enjoy the positive emotions associated with experiencing resolution rather than distress and overwhelm.

Listen to the recording for audio track 14.

Reflections

To what time in the near future, when your emotional flooding had subsided, were you able to fast-forward? How did your emotions change by fast-forwarding?

_____

_____

_____

_____

_____

What were some of the feelings you experienced after fast-forwarding?

_____

_____

_____

_____

_____

In what different scenarios do you anticipate using this tool in the future?

_____

_____

_____

_____

_____

 TOOL 10: JUXTAPOSITION OF TWO THOUGHTS OR FEELINGS

PURPOSE

— Recognize that contradictory, opposing thoughts or feelings can coexist.

— Learn to "hold" two opposing thoughts or feelings simultaneously, calling forth a counterpart to a distressing thought or feeling.

— Allow the positive counterpart to reduce the intensity of the opposing, negative thought or feeling you are experiencing.

— Experience the merging of the contradictory experiences and thoughts.

It's easy to become consumed by a powerful thought, emotion, or sensation. For example, if you've just twisted your ankle, the pain and throbbing most likely register front and center. Discomfort is all you feel and all you can think about. You hardly register the sensory input coming from the other, uninjured parts of your body. You are wired in such a way that the acute thoughts, feelings, or sensations you are experiencing trump the run-of-the-mill ones—even when that run-of-the-mill experience is one of well-being. This makes sense when you are physically injured or are facing any other type of threat. The heightened focus on the distressing sensation helps ensure that you attend to your injury or otherwise respond to the immediate threat. But what about those times when the acute distress originates from your thoughts or emotional experience, when your safety is not actually in jeopardy, but your emotions are responding as if it were?

When intense thoughts or emotions surge, Juxtaposition of Two Thoughts/Feelings gives you the freedom to access a broader range of thoughts or emotions. Rather than getting overcome by the intense experience, the juxtaposition exercise allows you to move between states of distress and well-being, calling upon a counterpart to your current thought/feeling. This has the effect of softening the overwhelming thoughts or emotions as well. So with this tool you gain the capacity to free yourself from any overwhelming thoughts or emotions, remembering that different thoughts or feelings not only exist but are yours to consider and experience whenever you wish.

DIRECTIONS

1. Remember a strong, aversive thought or feeling that you have experienced.
2. Imagine that you are placing this thought/emotion in the palm of one hand and make a fist to encapsulate this emotion and hold it there.
3. Now recognize that there's always an opposing thought/feeling that is available to you as well.
4. Direct your attention to one of these other, more positive thoughts or feelings.
5. Imagine that you are placing this thought or feeling in the palm of your other, free hand, making a fist to encapsulate it as well.
6. Now place your fists together so that the knuckles and base of your hands press together, letting the two thoughts/feelings coexist.
7. Bring your closed hands to your chest above your heart.
8. Experience the comfort and peace of mind of knowing that your contradictory thoughts or feelings can coexist.

Listen to the recording for audio track 15.

Reflections

Were you able to identify and access two opposing thoughts or feelings? Did calling up the positive, more affirming thought or feeling lessen the intensity of the negative thought/feeling? If so, what was this experience like for you?

_____

_____

_____

_____

How does the knowledge that a more positive thought/feeling is always available affect you?

_____

_____

_____

_____

Can you think of different scenarios in the future where you can use this tool? ·

_____

_____

_____

 TOOL 11: POSTPONEMENT

PURPOSE

— Develop the ability to put distressing thoughts, feelings, or impulses on hold.
— Postpone experiencing these thoughts, feelings, or impulses until a later, chosen time.
— Benefit from relegating distressing thoughts, feelings, or impulses to a time-limited window.

Everyone is familiar with the concept of postponement. The downside of postponement is procrastination—putting off something you don't want to do until a later time. On the other hand, postponement has a beneficial side. With Tool 11, you will learn to use postponement to put distressing thoughts, feelings, or impulses on hold. Used this way, postponement can help you manage worries and ruminative thoughts. Worries persistently dwell on the question "*what if*," holding your attention on an array of possible negative future outcomes. Ruminations are unrelenting, repetitive thoughts that cycle around and around in your head like a loop tape.

Postponement allows you to set a figurative snooze button on worried and ruminative thoughts, scheduling them for another time of your choice. When one such thought pops up, you can simply hit the snooze button, making a mental note that you'll allot time to attend to the thoughts later on in the day. You're not trying to banish your worries; rather, you are choosing to postpone giving them attention and to redirect your focus to what's relevant to the current moment. Postponement replaces a flat-out "no, don't think about that" command with "I'll create a time-limited window for attending to these worries."

The following exercise teaches you to engage in postponement. This includes scheduling a worry/rumination time at some point in your day when you will attend to the worry-ridden thoughts you've been postponing. This creates a win-win situation: You're postponing worried thoughts yet still taking time to give them attention. When your scheduled worry time arrives, you may prefer to spend it doing something else. However, honoring your commitment to your scheduled worry time strengthens your sense of control over ruminative thoughts and worries. You may discover that over time worry and rumination are taking up less mental energy and time in your day. Their power to command your time and attention significantly weakens as you practice the postponement tool.

DIRECTIONS

1. Notice any distressing thoughts, feelings, or impulses.
2. Temporarily put these thoughts, feeling, or impulses on hold, saying the word "stop" (either out loud or subvocally). *Optional: if you wish, you can also visualize a stop sign or make a hand gesture that indicates stop.*
3. Commit to revisit these worried and ruminative thoughts at a chosen time in the near future (often people choose to do so later that same day).

Listen to the recording for audio track 16.

Reflections

What place and time did you choose for your "worry/rumination time?"

_____

_____

_____

_____

What phrase, gesture, and/or visualization best helps you put the distressing thought/feeling/impulse on hold?

_____

_____

_____

_____

What are some of the challenges in postponing your distressing thoughts/feelings/impulses?

_____

_____

_____

_____

Can you think of different situations in the future where you can use this tool?

_____

_____

_____

_____

TOOL 12: SELF-STATEMENTS

PURPOSE

— Harness the power of your words.

— Recognize and affirm that you are capable of overcoming emotional reactivity.

— Face situations that are challenging or intimidating.

— Identify and engage thoughts that bring about empowerment.

Just as our thoughts can play a significant role in fueling emotional flooding, they can play an equally powerful role in quelling it. This is why the final tool in *every* time-out is self-statements. Words color your perception of your current experience, affect your memories, and solidify expectations of the future. Words build intentions— intentions regarding your ability to modulate your emotions in the present and intentions regarding how you will respond to triggers in the future.

With Tool 12, you harness the power of words with the use of self-statements. These self-statements affirm your ability to handle whatever triggers you, manage your life, and stop emotional flooding.

For this reason, the audio guide for Tool 12 contains prompts for you to insert whatever self-statement you need in the moment. By the end of the workbook, you will have self-statements that are both individualized and customized for each challenge you might encounter.

DIRECTIONS

1. Acknowledge the power of intention.
2. Acknowledge the power of the words that you say to yourself.
3. Say the affirming self-statements you have prepared for the particular challenge you are facing.

Listen to the recording for audio track 17.

Reflections

How have you noticed that your thoughts affect your experience and outlook? How does being around a friend or acquaintance who is chronically negative affect you? What is it like being around a friend or acquaintance who has a more optimistic and positive outlook?

_____

_____

_____

_____

How does your own, internal negative running commentary affect your mood? What about your own positive running commentary?

_____

_____

_____

_____

In what different scenarios in the future might you use this tool?

_____

_____

_____

_____

Take-Away Points

— Become familiar with the purpose and procedures for each of the 12 tools.

— Identify different scenarios in the future when you will anticipate using the tools.

— Use the audio recordings to familiarize yourself with and practice the 12 tools.

— Remember there's always a wise part of yourself that can handle a more vulnerable or reactive part.

Identifying and Managing Emotional Stressors: The STOP Solution ("P")

THIS CHAPTER PRESENTS APPLICATIONS OF THE 12 TOOLS TO DE-ESCALATE emotional flooding due to situational stressors or internal turmoil. Now that you've learned the 12 tools in Chapter 6, you can *Put the tools into practice* during your time-outs with the tool sets presented in this chapter and the next. Each stressor addressed in Chapters 7 and 8 is accompanied by a set of tools that is geared to de-escalate the accompanying emotional flooding, along with space for you to write about your use of these tools.

Each of the stressors in this chapter and the next also has a corresponding audio track that takes you through the entire tool set—including the Eye Roll, Tight Fist, and Focusing on the Breath (the "O" in "STOP")—for that trigger. Once you're in your time-out, you need only to access the audio track for the relevant trigger, and the "O" and "P" tools will play automatically. We suggest that you download these audio tracks (tracks 18–33) or use the Premium version of the workbook's companion app so that you can access the audio recordings whenever and wherever you take a time-out to engage the STOP Solution. With repeated practice of the tool sets you may become so familiar with the recordings that you discover you can easily elicit the desired state without playing the recording every time you feel the need to curtail emotional flooding.

The STOP Solution			
Scan	**T**ake	**O**vercome	**P**ut
your thoughts, emotions, behaviors, and sensations	a time-out	initial flooding	the tools into practice

COMMON EMOTIONAL TRIGGERS

— Worry

— Panic

— Intolerance of physical discomfort or distress

— Fear of abandonment/loneliness

— Hopelessness

— Frustration

— Explosive anger

Adapting the Tools to Work Best for You

The guidelines presented next give you a framework for gaining maximum benefit from the tools. All 12 tools reduce emotional flooding. However, some tools work better to address a particular trigger. That is why we've created this menu of suggested tools geared to each trigger. Although we've grouped the tool sets for each trigger into audio tracks for your convenience, we encourage you to substitute any tool that works better for you in a particular situation. For example, for panic you might prefer to use Tool 3 instead of Tool 8. If you'd prefer to implement the tool sets in a different order, we encourage you to do so as well. If you'd like to individualize the tools sets in any way, simply load each relevant track separately onto your audio device and cue the tracks accordingly. As you continue to select tools that work for you, you will develop a sense of what best eases your flooding.

The more you engage the tools, the more effective they become. As such, you may find that your emotional flooding sometimes dissipates before you complete the full tool set for a given trigger. If this is the case, feel free to skip to your self-statements to wrap-up your time-out. The more effectively you quell your emotional flooding as time goes on, the better. Over time, each tool you engage becomes more potent, and emotional flooding becomes less of the juggernaut than it once was.

WHEN MORE THAN ONE EMOTION IS PRESENT

Often, more than one triggering emotion occurs at the same time. For example, you might experience worry and frustration concurrently. In fact, you become more vulnerable to other triggers of flooding when you are already emotionally overwhelmed. When this occurs, address the emotion that is most intense first, the one that is at the forefront of your mind. If the emotions feel equally intense, arbitrarily pick one to address first. It is more important to engage a tool that will quickly de-escalate your activation than to spend much time deliberating over which tool set to apply first.

IDENTIFYING YOUR FREQUENT OFFENDERS

Each of the stressors covered in this chapter may trigger heightened emotions. Therefore, all of the tools presented can be useful. Some triggers, however, fall into the category of *frequent offenders*. As the name suggests, these are the triggers that most frequently elicit emotional flooding for you. As you read through the triggers listed here and throughout the chapter, put a checkmark in the box next to those that qualify as a frequent offender for you. By the time you're done, you will have a list of your frequent offenders.

MY FREQUENT OFFENDERS ────────────────────────

☐ Worry

☐ Panic

☐ Intolerance of physical discomfort or distress

☐ Fear of abandonment/loneliness

☐ Hopelessness

☐ Frustration

☐ Explosive anger

MANAGING YOUR FREQUENT OFFENDERS

We suggest keeping a list of your frequent offenders and their accompanying tools and audio tracks handy. Technology makes this easier. If you download the free companion app for this workbook, you will have easy access to a list of triggers and their corresponding audio track numbers on your smartphone. Alternately, you could keep a handwritten list of the triggers and their audio tracks in your purse or wallet. This way, when you are in the middle of emotional flooding and STOP for a time-out, you can quickly pull up the tools and the audio tracks that you need to play. No matter where you keep your list, the key is to have it and the accompanying audio tracks easily available when you need them.

GENERATING SELF-STATEMENTS

All the tools in this workbook end by using Tool 12, Self-Statements, as the final aspect of de-escalating emotional flooding. Remember, your words have power to fuel emotional flooding as well as to ease it. Self-statements are an essential tool to cement your de-escalation of emotional flooding and to close your time-out. Tool 12 prepares you to reengage in your daily activities with confidence and a sense of well-being.

Self-statements are most effective when they are individualized and address the specific challenge. For this reason you will be guided to create positive self-statements for each of the emotional challenges addressed in this workbook, which we suggest keeping with you for use during your time-outs. If you download the free companion app for this workbook, you will be able to input your custom self-statements for each trigger directly into the app so you can easily access them on the go. If you haven't already downloaded The Road to Calm Companion App from the Google Play or Apple App Store, we suggest doing so now.

The Tools for Inner Turmoil

WORRY

It's only human to worry occasionally. Worry can sometimes work to your benefit, motivating you to foresee the many possible outcomes of a situation and plan for different contingencies. However, worry becomes a problem when it is frequent and intense and robs you of the ability to enjoy the present moment. Worry pushes your focus into the future, anticipating what might possibly go wrong.

When you are stuck in worry, we recommend you STOP to use the following tools.

Suggested Tool Set				
WORRY Audio Track 18	Tool 1 Mindfulness with Detached Observation, p. 83	Tool 3 Dialing Down Reactivity, p. 88	Tool 11 Postponement, p. 105	Tool 12 Self-Statements, p. 108

Generating Self-Statements: Worry

To generate self-statements for worry, explore how you experience it. Recall a time when worried thoughts were racing through your mind. What were the barrage of thoughts that streamed through your mind when you were flooded with worry? For example, you might have thought, "This is never going to be okay"; "I'm trapped; this is never going to end." Write down a few of your thoughts in the space provided. Feel free to use the examples given.

Thought 1:

_____

Thought 2:

_____

Thought 3:

_____

Thought 4:

_____

Thought 5:

_____

You can use the thoughts you've written to generate the affirming self-statements you will use in Tool 12 to de-escalate worry. Simply write a compassionate, reassuring statement to challenge each of your flooding-immersed thoughts. In doing so, remember that you have a vast array of inner resources to tap into that often are overlooked when flooding is present. For example, "This is merely an aggravation, not a catastrophe," "This too will pass," "There isn't much evidence to support this worry," or "I can make a contingency plan in the unlikely event this happens."

Statement 1:

_____

Statement 2:

_____

Statement 3:

_____

Statement 4:

_____

Statement 5:

_____

Now that you have a list of individualized self-statements for worry, pick the three that feel the most powerful, meaningful, or helpful to you. You now have your worry-related self-statements for Tool 12. It can also be helpful to transfer them to a note that you can keep with you or enter them into this workbook's companion app on your phone so you'll have easy access whenever and wherever you need them.

Reflections

What was your experience as you generated your self-statements for worry?

_____

_____

_____

_____

In what future situations do you imagine yourself applying the self-statements?

_____

_____

_____

_____

PANIC (ESPECIALLY RELEVANT TO PANIC ATTACKS, PANIC DISORDER, AND POST TRAUMATIC STRESS DISORDER)

The experience of physical distress that occurs during a panic attack can be excruciating. Equally distressing are the worried thoughts that narrate (and often escalate) the panic. The meaning you give to your physical symptoms that accompany the panic, such as rapid heart rate or dizziness, losing control, or worse yet, going crazy, can make all the difference in preventing the escalation of your panic. The challenge for panic attack sufferers is the intolerance of the physical symptoms that typically accompany panic. You need to trust the reality that your body's inevitable reactions to panic do not bode catastrophe or serious harm to the body. They may be intensely uncomfortable, but they are transient. They will pass. Indeed, if you worry about these physical reactions, your worry further fuels the physiological panic response.

When you are stuck in panic, we recommend you STOP to use the tools that follow.

Suggested Tool Set				
PANIC Audio Track 19	Tool 1 Mindfulness with Detached Observation, p. 83	Tool 4 Heavy Hands, Heavy Legs, p. 91	Tool 9 Positive Future-Focusing, p. 101	Tool 12 Self-Statements, p. 108

Generating Self-Statements: Panic

To generate self-statements for panic, recall a time when feelings of panic were very strong for you. Notice the barrage of thoughts that ran through your mind when you were flooded with panic. For example, you might think, "I can't cope with this!"; "This is never going to be okay"; "I'm trapped and don't know what to do." Write down a few of your thoughts in the space provided. Feel free to use the examples given.

Thought 1:

_____

Thought 2:

_____

Thought 3:

_____

Thought 4:

_____

Thought 5:

_____

Now, you can use the thoughts you've written to generate the self-statements you can use in Tool 12 to de-escalate panic-related emotional flooding. To do so, simply write the opposite of each of your flooding-immersed thoughts. For example, you might write, "I can tolerate this," "I'm going to be okay soon," or "I'm not powerless. I know how to reduce the intensity of the panic." Feel free to use the examples given.

Statement 1:

_____

Statement 2:

_____

Statement 3:

_____

Statement 4:

_____

Statement 5:

_____

Now that you have a list of individualized self-statements for panic, pick the three that feel the most powerful, meaningful, or helpful to you. These are your panic-related self-statements for Tool 12. It can also be helpful to transfer them to a note that you can keep with you or enter them into this workbook's companion app on your phone so you'll have easy access whenever and wherever you need them.

Note: Asking yourself the question, "So what?" can also be very helpful. Think of the situations that most frighten you when you anticipate a panic attack. In the space that follows, use those situations to create "So what" questions for yourself and then answer them. For example, _So what if I have to run out of the grocery line with a full cart of food? I'll be embarrassed, but I'll get over it._

Or, *So what if I feel chest pain during a panic attack? If necessary, I'll go to the emergency room and get checked out.*

So what if _____

So what if _____

So what if _____

So what if _____

INTOLERANCE OF BODILY DISCOMFORT OR DISTRESS (ESPECIALLY RELEVANT FOR GENERALIZED ANXIETY DISORDER AND PANIC DISORDER)

Your brain is constantly receiving information from sensory neurons throughout your body—messages relating the numerous sensations that various parts of your body are experiencing. The vast majority of this sensory input does not reach conscious awareness. Some people, however, are more prone to noticing sensory input than others. This sensitivity can lead to both heightened physical discomfort and emotional distress. If you are prone to reacting to sensory input, a twinge of nausea that might not even register for someone else can hijack your attention and be very disturbing.

The process of heightened distress follows a typical sequence:

1. If you suffer from anxiety, your body responds with uncomfortable physical sensations.
2. Once you notice the sensations, it's very hard to ignore them.
3. Then you begin to scan for other uncomfortable sensations.
4. You begin to worry that the discomfort indicates that something is seriously wrong with your body.
5. The worry increases your stress levels and intensifies your emotional and physical discomfort.

It is possible to successfully combat this onslaught of distress and anxiety. Applying the following tool set will help you tolerate the physical discomforts that accompany emotional flooding and eliminate the worry that follows.

When you are flooded in response to feelings of physical discomfort or distress, we recommend you STOP to use the following tools.

Suggested Tool Set				
INTOLERANCE OF BODILY DISTRESS Audio Track 20	Tool 1 Mindfulness with Detached Observation, p. 83	Tool 2 Okay Signal, p. 85	Tool 4 Heavy Hands, Heavy Legs, p. 91	Tool 12 Self-Statements, p. 108

Generating Self-Statements: Intolerance of Bodily Discomfort or Distress

To generate self-statements for intolerance of physical discomfort or distress, recall a time when feelings of bodily distress were very strong for you. Notice the thoughts that streamed through your mind when you were flooded with these feelings. For example, you might have thought, "I can't stand this; I can't handle this; this is never going to end; this is a sign that something is seriously wrong with me." Write down a few of your thoughts in the space provided. Feel free to use the examples given.

Thought 1:

_____

Thought 2:

_____

Thought 3:

_____

Thought 4:

_____

Thought 5:

_____

Now, you can use the thoughts you've written to generate the self-state-ments for Tool 12 to de-escalate bodily-related emotional flooding. To do so, simply write the opposite of each of the thoughts. For example: "I can endure this," "These feelings are transient," "It's unlikely that there's any-thing seriously wrong with me," or "I'm not in danger." Feel free to use any of the examples also.

Statement 1:

_____

Statement 2:

_____

Statement 3:

_____

Statement 4:

_____

Statement 5:

_____

Now that you have a list of individualized self-statements for bodily dis-comfort, pick the three that feel the most powerful, meaningful, or helpful to you. You now have your bodily distress-related self-statements for Tool 12. It can also be helpful to transfer them to a note that you can keep with you or enter them into this workbook's companion app on your phone so you'll have easy access whenever and wherever you need them.

Reflections

What are the particular physical sensations that tend to frighten you?

_____

_____

_____

_____

Are there instances in the past when you've felt concern that your bodily symptoms indicated something was seriously wrong, and you turned out to be just fine? What do you remember about these experiences?

_____

_____

_____

_____

In what future circumstances might you use the self-statements you created? Provide as much detail as you can.

_____

_____

_____

_____

LONELINESS (ESPECIALLY RELEVANT FOR DEPRESSION AND ANXIETY)

We are evolutionarily engineered to live in communities, derive nourishment from engagement with one another, and form powerful attachments with family and close friends. The presence and quality of the close relationships in your lives can, in fact, bolster your ability to respond to stressors and regulate your emotions. In other words, when you have social support and close relationships, you are less prone to experiencing emotional flooding. Experiencing connection with others is a resource that can modulate the intensity of your distress.

Loneliness can arise from feeling isolated, forgotten, or uncared for. It's possible to feel lonely even in a relationship, if you perceive a lack of connection. No matter the cause, when you feel lonely, you are less capable of regulating your emotions and more susceptible to emotional flooding. It is for this reason that it is crucial to have tools to cope with feelings of loneliness.

One way you can lessen the amount of loneliness you experience is by creating and sustaining nourishing emotional bonds. However, even when these bonds exist, you can still become flooded with feelings of loneliness. This is when you can use the tools to invoke the feelings of safety, comfort, and well-being that connection with others brings. There are two keys to decreasing loneliness: developing and maintaining positive relationships; and remembering the satisfying emotions that these relationships bring, whether you are alone or with others.

When you are flooded with feelings of loneliness, we recommend you STOP to use the following tools.

Suggested Tool Set				
LONELINESS Audio Track 21	Tool 5 Imaginary Support Circle, p. 93	Tool 6 Wise Self, p. 95	Tool 10 Juxta-position of Two Thoughts or Feelings, p. 103	Tool 12 Self-Statements, p. 108

Generating Self-Statements: Loneliness

To generate self-statements for loneliness, recall a time when feelings of loneliness were particularly strong. Notice the thoughts on your mind when you were flooded with loneliness. For example, you might have thought, "No one is truly there for me," "Everyone eventually will leave me," or "I don't have anyone in my life." Write down a few of your thoughts in the space provided. Feel free to use any of the examples given.

Thought 1:

_____

Thought 2:

_____

Thought 3:

_____

Thought 4:

_____

Thought 5:

_____

Now, use the thoughts you've written to generate the self-statements you can use in Tool 12 to de-escalate loneliness-related emotional flooding. To do so, simply write the opposite of each of your flooding-immersed thoughts. For example: "I do have people in my life who care about me," or "It's possible that some people will leave me, but I know that not everyone will leave me." Feel free to use any of the examples also.

Statement 1:

_____

Statement 2:

_____

Statement 3:

_____

Statement 4:

_____

Statement 5:

_____

Now that you have a list of individualized self-statements for loneliness and a few commonly used ones, pick the three that feel the most powerful, meaningful, or helpful to you. You now have your fear of loneliness-related self-statements for Tool 12. It can also be helpful to transfer them to a note that you can keep with you or enter them into this workbook's companion app on your phone so you'll have easy access whenever and wherever you need them.

Reflections

Describe the memory you elicited that brought up strong feelings of loneliness.

_____
_____
_____

Do you have a memory from your childhood of feeling particularly lonely? If so, what is it?

_____
_____
_____

In what future situations might you use the self-statements you've created?

_____
_____
_____

PERVASIVE HOPELESSNESS (ESPECIALLY RELEVANT FOR DEPRESSION AND PTSD)

The internal self-talk that supports pervasive hopelessness comes from a steadfast belief that everything you do or hope for is futile; that no matter what you do, things will turn out badly; that it's pointless to take action because nothing ever works. Feelings of emotional numbness and/or despair also often accompany pervasive hopelessness.

Hopelessness and inaction are strongly linked. When hopelessness is present, it can feel nearly impossible to take action. This is because, with hopelessness, the body and mind enter into a state of immobilization. Unlike states of panic or rage, in which your heart races and you are too energized, hopelessness is experienced as a precipitous drop in energy. Despite the lack of energy, pervasive hopelessness is another type of emotional flooding.

When you are flooded with feelings of hopelessness, we recommend you STOP to use the following tools.

Given the lack of energy that accompanies hopelessness, engaging the tools listed here might pose a challenge because they require action, and you might be pessimistic about their effectiveness. We suggest that you suspend your sense of futility for the moment and engage, *no matter what* and regardless of your energy levels, in the following tools.

Suggested Tool Set				
HOPELESSNESS Audio Track 22	Tool 8 Remembering Successes, p. 99	Tool 6 Wise Self, p. 95	Tool 9 Positive Future-Focusing, p. 101	Tool 12 Self-Statements, p. 108

Generating Self-Statements: Hopelessness

To generate self-statements for hopelessness, recall a time when feelings of hopelessness were particularly strong. Notice your thoughts when you are flooded with those feelings. For example, you might think, "Nothing is going to help," "I want to but don't have the energy to," or "There's no way out of this for me." Write down a few of your thoughts in the space provided. Feel free to use the examples given.

Thought 1:

_____

Thought 2:

_____

Thought 3:

_____

Thought 4:

_____

Thought 5:

_____

Now, you can use the thoughts you've written to generate the self-statements in Tool 12 to de-escalate hopeless-related emotional flooding. To do so, simply write the opposite of each of your flooding-immersed thoughts. For example, "If I am persistent with the tools, some of them will help me," "I may not feel like doing this, but I know it's in my best interest," "I can do this even though I feel like I have no energy," and "There's almost always a solution, I just need to be open to possibilities."

Statement 1:

_____

Statement 2:

_____

Statement 3:

_____

Statement 4:

_____

Statement 5:

_____

Now that you have a list of individualized self-statements for hopelessness, pick the three that feel the most powerful, meaningful, or helpful to you. You now have your hopelessness-related self-statements for Tool 12. It can also be helpful to transfer them to a note that you can keep with you or enter them into this workbook's companion app on your phone so you'll have easy access whenever and wherever you need them.

Reflections

Describe a circumstance when you felt particularly hopeless. What were the details of that experience?

_____

_____

_____

Think of a time when it was difficult for you to gather the energy to do something that a part of you knew you should do. Describe the situation and what you did or didn't do.

_____

_____

_____

In the instance just described, if you were able to overcome inaction, what strategies did you use?

_____

_____

_____

Did anyone support your efforts?

_____

In what circumstances in the future might you use the self-statements you have created?

_____

_____

_____

INTOLERABLE FRUSTRATION

When it becomes intolerable, frustration can be a particularly insidious trigger of emotional dysregulation. If you have low frustration tolerance you can be flooded by what seems to others like minor aggravations. Your frustrations can pile up as well, each adding to your experience of emotional overwhelm. In this way frustrations can have a cumulative effect. A frustration that might not normally send you into overwhelm can bring you to the boiling point if you are already frustrated by another circumstance. Further, if you have low frustration tolerance it's easy to focus on and ruminate about the unfairness of frustrating situations, and these ruminations alone can trigger emotional flooding. For these reasons, it's important to take a time-out and implement the tools to de-escalate intolerable frustration when you first notice it arising.

When you are stuck in feelings of frustration, we recommend you STOP to use the following tools. If your day is particularly stressful (and especially if you are also physically depleted), we recommend that you plan on engaging the tools several times throughout the day.

Suggested Tool Set				
FRUSTRATION Audio Track 23	Tool 3 Dialing Down Reactivity, p. 88	Tool 2 Okay Signal, p. 85	Tool 6 Wise Self, p. 95	Tool 12 Self-Statements, p. 108

Generating Self-Statements: Intolerable Frustration

To generate self-statements for frustration, recall a time when feelings of frustration were particularly strong. Notice your thoughts when you were flooded with those feelings. For example, you might have thought, "I can't stand how long this is taking"; "This is totally unfair!"; "How could they be so stupid!" Write down a few of your thoughts in the space provided. Feel free to use the examples given.

Thought 1:

_____

Thought 2:

_____

Thought 3:

_____

Thought 4:

_____

Thought 5:

_____

Now, you can use the thoughts you've written to generate the self-statements you can use in Tool 12 to de-escalate frustration-related emotional flooding. To do so, simply write the opposite of each of your flooding-immersed thoughts. It doesn't have to be a literal opposite, but an alternative view of the situation. For example, "I accept that things are not always fair"; "I may not like waiting, but I can use the time to self-soothe"; or "I choose to be curious about the person who annoyed me." Feel free to use any of these examples also.

Statement 1:

_____

Statement 2:

_____

Statement 3:

_____

Statement 4:

_____

Statement 5:

_____

Now that you have a list of individualized self-statements for frustration, pick the three that feel the most powerful, meaningful, or helpful to you. You now have your frustration-related self-statements for Tool 12. It can also be helpful to transfer them to a note that you can keep with you or enter them into this workbook's companion app on your phone so you'll have easy access whenever and wherever you need them.

Reflections
Describe the circumstances of the frustrating situation that you recalled.

_____

_____

_____

_____

_____

Are there particular circumstances that you find more frustrating than others? If so, what are they?

_____

_____

_____

What personality characteristics (for example, controlling, selfish, rigid, etc.) frustrate you and how have you dealt with this in the past?

_____

_____

_____

In what future circumstances might you use these self-statements?

_____

_____

_____

EXPLOSIVE ANGER (ESPECIALLY RELEVANT FOR INTERMITTENT EXPLOSIVE DISORDER)

Like emotional flooding related to panic, the onset of explosive anger is both sudden and strong. "Going through the roof"; "losing your head"; "boiling over with rage"; and "erupting; exploding" are commonly used metaphors for explosive anger. As these metaphors reflect, anger can quickly surge from within, overpowering any attempts to restrain it. Explosive anger carries with it a firestorm of physiological activation. Your heart rate quickens, your blood rushes to your major muscle groups, giving them energy to fight, and hormones are released to energize the impulse to spring into action. These strong physiological responses that are part of explosive anger make it crucial to quickly implement the tools to contain this type of emotional flooding. It is essential to know your flooding profile for explosive anger (see Chapter 6) so you can quickly engage your time-out when the first signs of anger arise.

 When you are stuck in explosive anger, we recommend you STOP to use the following tools.

Note: Due to the intensity of this particular type of emotional flooding, you may need to run through the tools multiple times during a single time-out. Each run-through of the tools will increasingly lower your level of activation. Be sure not to end your time-out until the anger has *fully* dissipated. Cutting the process short can make your time-out ineffective.

Suggested Tool Set				
EXPLOSIVE ANGER Audio Track 24	Tool 4 Heavy Hands, Heavy Legs, p. 91	Tool 3 Dialing Down Reactivity, p. 88	Tool 6 Wise Self, p. 95	Tool 12 Self-Statements, p. 108

Generating Self-Statements: Explosive Anger

To generate self-statements for explosive anger, recall a time when feelings of explosive anger or rage were particularly strong. Notice your thoughts when you were flooded with those feelings. For example, you might have thought, "I could kill somebody!"; "Who do you think you are!"; "I'll get back at them for this!" Write down a few of your thoughts in the space provided. Feel free to use the examples given.

Thought 1:
_____

Thought 2:
_____

Thought 3:
_____

Thought 4:
_____

Thought 5:
_____

Now use the thoughts you've written to generate the self-statements you can use in Tool 12 to de-escalate explosive anger-related emotional flooding. To do so, simply write the opposite of or alternative to each of your flooding-immersed thoughts. For example, "I'm upset but I can handle it," "I don't have to take action now," or "I can think before I respond." Feel free to use any of the earlier examples also.

Statement 1:

_____

Statement 2:

_____

Statement 3:

_____

Statement 4:

_____

Statement 5:

_____

Now that you have a list of individualized self-statements for explosive anger, pick the three that feel the most powerful, meaningful, or helpful to you. You now have your explosive anger-related self-statements for Tool 12. It can also be helpful to transfer them to a note that you can keep with you or enter them into this workbook's companion app on your phone so you'll have easy access whenever and wherever you need them.

Reflections
What memory did you recall? How did you handle it?

_____

Are there specific circumstances that predictably cause explosive anger for you? If so, what are they?

_____

_____

_____

In what future circumstances might you use the self-statements you created? Provide as much detail as you can.

_____

_____

_____

Take-Away Points

— Know your frequent offenders and use this workbook's Premium companion app or a portable audio device to keep the audio tracks containing the tool sets (tracks 18–33) handy at all times.

— When you are triggered by one emotion, you are more vulnerable to being triggered by other emotions. Use the tools appropriate to each trigger.

— Take care to practice all the tools, with special attention directed toward the tools for each of your frequent offenders.

— Affirming self-statements can diminish your reactivity.

— Keep your self-statements for all triggers, and especially your frequent offenders, handy by using The Road to Calm Companion App or carrying them with you on a sheet of paper.

— Make a copy of the following table, take a picture that you store in your smartphone, or download The Road to Calm Companion App to keep this information with you at all times:

Suggested Tool Sets for Managing Emotional Stressors			
WORRY Audio Track 18	Tool 1 Mindfulness with Detached Observation, p. 83	Tool 3 Dialing Down Reactivity, p. 88	Tool 11 Postponement, p. 105	Tool 12 Self-Statements, p. 108
PANIC Audio Track 19	Tool 1 Mindfulness with Detached Observation, p. 83	Tool 4 Heavy Hands, Heavy Legs, p. 91	Tool 9 Positive Future-Focusing, p. 101	Tool 12 Self-Statements, p. 108
INTOLERANCE OF BODILY DISTRESS Audio Track 20	Tool 1 Mindfulness with Detached Observation, p. 83	Tool 2 Okay Signal, p. 85	Tool 4 Heavy Hands, Heavy Legs, p. 91	Tool 12 Self-Statements, p. 108
LONELINESS Audio Track 21	Tool 5 Imaginary Support Circle, p. 93	Tool 6 Wise Self, p. 95	Tool 10 Juxta-position of Two Thoughts or Feel-ings, p. 103	Tool 12 Self-Statements, p. 108
HOPELESSNESS Audio Track 22	Tool 8 Remembering Successes, p. 99	Tool 6 Wise Self, p. 95	Tool 9 Positive Future-Focusing, p. 101	Tool 12 Self-Statements, p. 108
FRUSTRATION Audio Track 23	Tool 3 Dialing Down Reactivity, p. 88	Tool 2 Okay Signal, p. 85	Tool 6 Wise Self, p. 95	Tool 12 Self-Statements, p. 108
EXPLOSIVE ANGER Audio Track 24	Tool 4 Heavy Hands, Heavy Legs, p. 91	Tool 3 Dialing Down Reactivity, p. 88	Tool 6 Wise Self, p. 95	Tool 12 Self-Statements, p. 108

8 Managing Emotional Flooding in Relationships: The STOP Solution ("P")

Your task is not to seek love, but to seek and find all the barriers within yourself that you have built against it.

—RUMI

EVEN THE BEST RELATIONSHIPS INEVITABLY TRIGGER INTENSE EMOTIONAL reactions at times. How you respond to those triggers may determine the fate of your relationships. This chapter shows you how to use the tools to reduce emotional flooding and resolve relationship conflicts. Following the initial three steps of the time-out, you can proceed with the tool set specifically designed to help you navigate the relational stressor that is troubling you in the moment.

The STOP Solution			
Scan your thoughts, emotions, behaviors, and sensations	**T**ake a time-out	**O**vercome initial flooding	**P**ut the tools into practice

In this chapter, you will learn how to STOP and Put the tools into practice for the following interpersonal triggers:

— abandonment
— betrayal

- feeling controlled
- criticism
- feeling judged/shamed
- feeling misunderstood
- feeling lack of empathy toward you
- resentment
- feeling defeated/hopeless

"We can be serene even in the midst of calamities and, by our serenity, make others more tranquil."

—SWAMI SATCHIDANANDA

As in Chapter 7, each of the stressors in this chapter has a corresponding audio track that takes you through the entire suggested tool set—including the Eye Roll, Tight Fist, and Focusing on the Breath (the "O" in "STOP")—for that trigger. Once you're in your time-out, you can access the audio track for the relevant trigger and the "O" and "P" tools will play automatically. We suggest that you download these audio tracks (tracks 18–33) or use the Premium version of the workbook's companion app to access the audio recordings whenever and wherever you need to take a time-out.

You'll also recall from Chapter 7 that every tool in this workbook ends with Tool 12, Self-Statements. Self-statements are most powerful if they are individualized and specifically address the challenge at hand. For this reason you will be guided to create positive self-statements for each of the emotional challenges addressed in this chapter, which we suggest keeping with you for use during your time-outs. (You may find it helpful to review the section *Generating Self-Statements* in Chapter 7.)

The Tools for Interpersonal Triggers

FEELING ABANDONED

Living as part of a family or community is key to your survival. If the young are not closely tended to, they will die. The bigger the herd you belong to and associate with, the more likely you are to have your physical and emotional needs met, and the less vulnerable you are to environmental threats. It is for this reason that you have the built-in instinct to nurture your young, to nurture connection with one another, and to form community. Abandonment can bring death.

In many early human societies—and in some today—the most severe form of punishment was banishment from family or community. It meant loss of the protection of the tribe, the common bonds, and the strength in numbers a tribe provides. Banishment results in great emotional suffering: having to live in the absence of the community you were raised in, and without those you love. Shakespeare drew a strong parallel between banishment and death in *Romeo and Juliet*. Romeo bewails his banishment from Verona, stating that banishment is simply "death mis-term'd."

The importance of community and a feeling of belonging explain why the feeling of abandonment—a deep, primal sense of loss and separation—can trigger intense emotional flooding. You feel unwanted and alone. Your ability to survive in the world feels threatened. This is why the withdrawal of emotional connection can set off alarm bells and lead to emotional flooding.

When you are overwhelmed by feelings of being abandoned in a relationship, we recommend you STOP to use the following tools.

Suggested Tool Set				
FEELING ABANDONED Audio Track 25	Tool 1 Mindfulness with Detached Observation, p. 83	Tool 6 Wise Self, p. 95	Tool 7 Empathic Self, p. 97	Tool 12 Self-Statements, p. 108

Generating Self-Statements: Feeling Abandoned

To generate self-statements related to feelings of abandonment, recall a time when you experienced abandonment. Notice your thoughts when you were flooded by feelings of abandonment. For example, you might have thought to yourself, "I am all alone," or "I can't survive without . . .," "The meaning of my life is gone." Write down your thoughts when you feel abandoned on the lines that follow. Feel free to use any of the examples.

Thought 1:

_____

Thought 2:

_____

Thought 3:

_____

Thought 4:

_____

Thought 5:

_____

Now, you can use the thoughts you've written to generate the self-statements used in Tool 12 to de-escalate abandonment-related emotional flooding. To do so, write a compassionate, reassuring statements in response to each of the thoughts. Examples of positive self-statements might be, "When I stop to think about it, I see that there _are_ other people in my life"; "Even though I'd like things to be different, I can survive"; or "The quality of my life isn't dependent on one person." Feel free to use any of the examples.

Statement 1:

_____

Statement 2:

_____

Statement 3:

_____

Statement 4:

_____

Statement 5:

_____

Now that you have a list of individualized self-statements for feeling abandoned, pick the three that feel the most powerful, meaningful, or helpful to you. You now have your abandonment-related self-statements for Tool 12. It can also be helpful to transfer them to a note that you can keep with you or enter them into this workbook's companion app on your phone so you'll have easy access whenever and wherever you need them.

Reflections

Describe the situation you recalled when you felt abandoned.

_____
_____
_____

How did you respond to the feelings of abandonment?

_____
_____
_____

Do you have any memories from childhood of feelings of abandonment?

_____
_____
_____

In what future situations might you use the self-statements you've created? Be as specific as you can.

_____
_____
_____

FEELINGS OF BETRAYAL

Trust is a fundamental component of meaningful, life-enhancing relationships and is essential to life in a community. The more significant the relationship, the greater the degree of emotional trust needed and the greater the pain if that trust is betrayed. As you build trust in relationships, you increasingly reveal yourself—your fears, insecurities, hopes, and desires. The emotional trust you build provides a powerful sense of connection, safety, and well-being. A betrayal of this trust is, therefore, devastating.

Because people are flawed, feelings of betrayal can be pervasive in relationships. If betrayal is an emotional trigger for you, even what others might perceive as a minor insensitivity can feel to you like betrayal and cut you to the core. Any perceived betrayal of trust can be so profound that it leads to emotional flooding. This is why it is essential that you have tools to manage these intense feelings.

When you are overwhelmed by feelings of betrayal in a relationship, we recommend you STOP to use the following tools.

Suggested Tool Set				
FEELINGS OF BETRAYAL Audio Track 26	Tool 3 Dialing Down Reactivity, p. 88	Tool 7 Empathic Self, p. 97	Tool 9 Positive Future-Focusing, p. 101	Tool 12 Self-Statements, p. 107

Generating Self-Statements: Feelings of Betrayal

To generate self-statements for feelings of betrayal, recall a time when the feeling was particularly strong. Notice your thoughts when you were flooded with these feelings. For example, you might have thought, "I'm so disappointed he'd do that to me"; "I was a fool to trust her"; "I'm not strong enough to handle this break in trust." Write down a few of your thoughts in the space provided. Also feel free to use any of the examples given.

Thought 1:

_____

Thought 2:

_____

Thought 3:

_____

Thought 4:

_____

Thought 5:

_____

Now, you can use the thoughts you've written to generate the self-statements you can use in Tool 12 to de-escalate betrayal-related emotional flooding. To do so, write a compassionate, reassuring statement in response to each of the thoughts. Examples of positive statements might include: "Disappointment is natural in this circumstance, but it won't last forever"; "It's not appropriate to blame myself for this betrayal of trust"; "I can learn from this experience"; and "I am strong enough to face what has happened with courage." Also feel free to use any of the examples.

Statement 1:

_____

Statement 2:

_____

Statement 3:

_____

Statement 4:

Statement 5:

_____

Now that you have a list of individualized self-statements for responding to feelings of betrayal, pick the three that feel the most powerful, meaningful, or helpful to you. These are your betrayal-related self-statements for
Tool 12. It can also be helpful to transfer them to a note that you can keep
with you or enter them into this workbook's companion app on your phone
so you'll have easy access whenever and wherever you need them.

Reflections
Describe the feelings elicited when you recalled a betrayal.

_____

_____

_____

How did you handle your feelings in that situation?

_____

_____

_____

Do you remember experiencing feelings of betrayal in your childhood? If so,
describe them.

_____

_____

_____

In what future situations might you use the self-statements? Be as specific
as possible.

_____

FEELING CONTROLLED

In order to feel safe in the world, you need to be able to exercise your power to choose actions and decisions that influence your life. Babies are delighted when they figure out that by hitting a pile of blocks, they can make the blocks topple down. As an adult, your satisfaction and confidence grow as you exercise more control over your personal circumstances. The world would be a terrifying place if you were unable to take action or make decisions. Therefore, a threat to your sense of control in specific situations can trigger emotional flooding.

When you are stuck in feelings of being controlled in a relationship, we recommend you STOP to use the following tools.

Suggested Tool Set				
FEELING CONTROLLED Audio Track 27	Tool 1 Mindfulness with Detached Observation, p. 83	Tool 10 Juxta-position of Two Thoughts or Feelings, p. 103	Tool 3 Dialing Down Reactivity, p. 88	Tool 12 Self-Statements, p. 108

Generating Self-Statements: Feeling Controlled

You can begin by eliciting a memory of a time when you experienced feelings of being controlled. Notice your thoughts when you were flooded with these feelings. Choose a few of those thoughts and write them down on the lines that follow. For example, you might have thought, "Why can't I have a say in this?" "This person is trying to control me to do it her way"; "I feel coerced when they tell me what to do." Also feel free to use any of the examples.

Thought 1:

Thought 2:

_____

Thought 3:

_____

Thought 4:

_____

Thought 5:

_____

Now, use the thoughts you've written to generate the self-statements to use in Tool 12 to de-escalate emotional flooding due to feeling controlled. To do so, write a compassionate, reassuring statement in response to each of your thoughts. Examples of self-statements might include the following: "I have a right to have a say in decisions," "I have the courage to not be controlled," and "I can listen respectfully to their suggestion, but ultimately I make my own decisions." Also feel free to use any of the examples.

Statement 1:

_____

Statement 2:

_____

Statement 3:

_____

Statement 4:

_____

Statement 5:

_____

Now that you have a list of individualized self-statements for feeling controlled, pick the three that feel the most powerful, meaningful, or helpful to you. You now have your control-related self-statements for Tool 12. It can also be helpful to transfer them to a note that you can keep with you or enter them into this workbook's companion app on your phone so you'll have easy access whenever and wherever you need them.

Reflections
Describe the situation(s) you elicited that led you to feel controlled.

_____
_____
_____

Who in your life especially raises feelings of being controlled? How do you respond to them?

_____
_____
_____

In what specific situations can you imagine using the self-statements in the future?

_____
_____
_____

FEELING CRITICIZED
Constructive criticism is a natural part of any relationship, but even if you are not especially vulnerable to criticism, it can trigger emotional flooding when you are criticized in a manner that belittles you. And, if you have a history of being the object of ridicule or harsh and shaming criticism, you may

be particularly vulnerable to criticism. Further, some people who are perfectionists may be hypersensitive to criticism. In these cases, criticism may cause you to feel devalued and inferior, as if there were something wrong with you as a person. Your sense of self-worth feels threatened. When this occurs, feeling criticized can often trigger emotional flooding.

When you feel stuck in feelings of being criticized, we recommend you STOP to use the following tools.

Suggested Tool Set				
FEELING CRITICIZED Audio Track 28	Tool 8 Remembering Successes, p. 99	Tool 2 Okay Signal, p. 85	Tool 7 Empathic Self, p. 97	Tool 12 Self-Statements, p. 108

Generating Self-Statements: Feeling Criticized

Recall a time when you experienced a strong reaction to feeling criticized. Notice your thoughts when you were flooded with those feelings. For example, you might have thought, "Who do they think they are, criticizing me like that?" "I'm trying so hard to do well but she still criticizes me," or "How could I have done something so stupid?"

Choose a few of those thoughts and write them down on the lines that follow. Feel free to use the examples provided.

Thought 1:

_____

Thought 2:

_____

Thought 3:

_____

Thought 4:

Thought 5:

_____

Now, you can use the thoughts you've written to generate the self-statements for use in Tool 12 to de-escalate criticism-related emotional flooding. Simply write a compassionate, reassuring statement in response to each of your reactive thoughts. Examples of self-statements are as follows: "What can I learn from this feedback?"; "I'm doing the best I can. This may be more about her than me"; "I don't like making mistakes but I accept myself when I do"; and "Making mistakes is part of being human." Statement 1:

_____

Statement 2:

_____

Statement 3:

_____

Statement 4:

_____

Statement 5:

_____

Now that you have a list of individualized self-statements for criticism, pick the three that feel the most powerful, meaningful, or helpful to you. You now have your criticism-related self-statements for Tool 12. It can also be helpful to transfer them to a note that you can keep with you or enter them into this workbook's companion app on your phone so you'll have easy access whenever and wherever you need them.

Reflections

Describe the situation(s) you elicited that led you to feel criticized.

_____

_____

_____

Who in your life especially raises feelings of being criticized? How do you respond to them?

_____

_____

_____

In what specific situations can you imagine using the self-statements in the future?

_____

_____

_____

FEELING JUDGED OR SHAMED

Feeling judged results from a direct, intentional attack on your self-worth and value as a person. It is the personal nature of the attack that makes it distinct from criticism. Judgment is a pronouncement that conveys scorn, contempt, and the inferiority of another. It can cause you to feel devalued and inferior, as if there were something wrong with you at your core. When you overreact to judgment, you question your inherent worth, which triggers shame. Rather than delivering the message "I made a mistake," shame carries the deeper message, "I *am* the mistake, and I am fundamentally flawed." That assessment often triggers emotional flooding.

No one escapes judgment. Being embarrassed and experiencing the harsh disapproval of others is part of the human experience. For instance, you may have been ridiculed by your professor when you weren't prepared for class, or your boss expressed scorn for your work in front of your colleagues. No one likes to feel judged, but for some people, it contributes to an already overdeveloped sense of shame.

Because shame is so deeply rooted, the emotional flooding it can cause can be particularly powerful. This is especially true when the harsh judgment isn't immediately followed by the expression of a caring and validating connection, optimally with the person who made the judgment. Your nervous system is especially primed to experience emotional flooding in response to shame when, as children, the disapproval you received wasn't quickly followed by the reestablishment of caring, loving connection (Schore, 1996). Without the reengagement of connection, your developing nervous systems didn't get the experience of reregulating immediately following the jolt that occurred with shame. As a child, you needed to be taught how to explore the world safely. As an adult, your nervous system needs to be taught how to regulate after experiences of shame.

When you feel flooded with feelings of judgment and shame, we recommend you STOP to use the following tools.

"You yourself, as much as anybody in the entire universe, deserves your love and affection." —BUDDHA

Suggested Tool Set				
FEELING JUDGED/ SHAMED Audio Track 29	Tool 1 Mindfulness with Detached Observation, p. 83	Tool 2 Okay Signal, p. 85	Tool 6 Wise Self, p. 95	Tool 12 Self-Statements, p. 108

Generating Self-Statements: Feeling Judged or Shamed

Begin by tapping into the experience of feeling judged or shamed. You might call up a memory of a time when the feeling of being judged or shamed was particularly strong. Notice your thoughts when you were flooded with these feelings. Choose a few of those thoughts and write them down on the lines that follow. For example, you might write, "I am worthless," "There is no hope for my doing anything right," "I hurt," or "I'll always feel this way." Feel free to use the examples provided.

Thought 1:

_____

Thought 2:

_____

Thought 3:

_____

Thought 4:

_____

Thought 5:

_____

Now, you can use the thoughts you've written to generate the self-statements you can use in Tool 12 to de-escalate judgment-related emotional flooding. To do so, write a compassionate, reassuring statement in response to each of your flooding-immersed thoughts. For example, "I am okay," "I often do things well and will again," "I can have compassion for myself," or "I've already changed in many ways and I can make other changes as well."

Statement 1:

_____

Statement 2:

_____

Statement 3:

_____

Statement 4:

_____

Statement 5:

_____

Now that you have a list of individualized self-statements for feeling judged and a few commonly used ones, pick the three that feel the most powerful, meaningful, or helpful to you. You now have your judgment-related self-statements for Tool 12. It can also be helpful to transfer them to a note that you can keep with you or enter them into this workbook's companion app on your phone so you'll have easy access whenever and wherever you need them.

Reflections

Describe the situation(s) you elicited that led you to feel judged or shamed.

_____
_____
_____

Who in your life especially raises feelings of being judged or shamed? How do you respond to them?

_____
_____
_____

In what specific situations can you imagine using the self-statements in the future?

_____

FEELING MISUNDERSTOOD

"There is no worse lie than a truth misunderstood by those who hear it." —WILLIAM JAMES

Somebody once said, "I really don't mind being hated, but I really hate being misunderstood." You may have had the frustrating experience of thinking you've communicated clearly, yet the message you intended is misunderstood. There are several reasons this may happen. Sometimes the person to whom you are speaking may not have listened well. Other times the receiver of your communication responded on the basis of their preconceived—but inaccurate—assumptions about what you mean or what you are communicating.

Sometimes it's not your words that are misunderstood, but your actions. For instance, you offer well-meaning advice to a close friend who misunderstands your intentions and feels belittled. Or you have difficulty doing some mechanical or technical task and ask your spouse to teach you how to do it. Instead, your spouse misunderstands your request and takes over and does the task. Or you give feedback to a coworker on her writing, and she thinks you are trying to show that you are a much better writer than she. There are endless examples of situations in which you may have experienced trying to do something kind or helpful and had your actions misconstrued.

As we discussed in Chapter 3, attuned connection and emotional resonance occur when you experience being seen and felt by others. Indeed, Daniel Siegel (2007), psychiatrist, author, and expert in interpersonal neurobiology, observes that at the heart of an empathic relationship is the experience of sending a clear image of our mind to the mind of another. A key to being happy in relationships is to feel that the other person gets you. When you're misunderstood, the satisfaction in any relationship is temporarily broken, which may trigger emotional flooding. Feeling understood is essential to attuned connection. For these reasons feeling misunderstood can be deeply jarring.

When emotional flooding due to being misunderstood occurs, we recommend you STOP to use the following tools.

Suggested Tool Set				
FEELING MIS-UNDERSTOOD Audio Track 30	Tool 1 Mindfulness with Detached Observation, p. 83	Tool 7 Empathic Self, p. 97	Tool 10 Juxta-position of Two Thoughts or Feelings, p. 103	Tool 12 Self-Statements, p. 108

Generating Self-Statements: Feeling Misunderstood

Remember a time when you experienced a strong reaction to feeling misunderstood. Notice your thoughts when you were flooded with those feelings. For example, you might have thought, "How could they misunderstand me?" "Are you even listening to me?" "How can I possibly get through to you?" or "I'm so bad at explaining things clearly!"

Choose a few of your thoughts and write them down on the lines that follow. Feel free to use the earlier examples.

Thought 1:

_____

Thought 2:

_____

Thought 3:

_____

Thought 4:

_____

Thought 5:

_____

Now you can use the thoughts you've written to generate the self-statements to use in Tool 12 to de-escalate emotional flooding that comes from feeling misunderstood. To do so, write a compassionate, reassuring statement in response to each of your flooding-immersed thoughts. For example: "He may not be a good listener, but he has many endearing qualities." "I'm curious about another way I can explain it to her." "I often communicate so that people understand what I'm saying." Feel free to use the examples given.

Statement 1:

_____

Statement 2:

_____

Statement 3:

_____

Statement 4:

_____

Statement 5:

_____

Now that you have a list of individualized self-statements for feeling misunderstood, pick the three that feel the most powerful, meaningful, or helpful to you. You now have your self-statements related to feeling misunderstood for Tool 12. It can also be helpful to transfer them to a note that you can keep with you or enter them into this workbook's companion app on your phone so you'll have easy access whenever and wherever you need them.

Reflections

Describe the situation(s) you elicited that led you to feel misunderstood.

_____

_____

_____

Who in your life especially raises feelings of being misunderstood? How do you respond to them?

_____

_____

_____

In what specific situations can you imagine using the self-statements in the future?

_____

_____

_____

FEELING A LACK OF EMPATHY FROM ANOTHER

The feeling that someone close to you is indifferent to your pain because they don't offer empathy can be another cause of emotional flooding. We defined empathy in *Anxious in Love* as "the ability to identify with another's feelings and to emotionally put yourself in somebody else's shoes" (Daitch & Lorberbaum, 2012, p. 131). Of course, you can never experience exactly what another person is feeling. You can, however, emotionally tap in to the experience of another. "When you empathize you gain a sense of the emotional terrain of another's world . . . and you convey this understanding to [the other person]" (Daitch & Lorberbaum, 2012, p. 131). Harville Hendrix, PhD, marital therapist and author of *Getting the Love You Want,* corroborates this concept. He writes, "Empathy is the most powerful bonding experience you can have. It restores the experience of connectedness and union" (Hendrix, 2010, p. 3).

Your need for empathy goes back to infancy. Psychology research on attachment makes it clear that an infant's secure attachment results in large part from the caregiver's empathic sensitivity. The research shows both the innate need for empathy and the impact on the developing child when empathy is lacking. Insufficient empathy in your early years can continue to affect you as you grow from childhood to adolescence and adulthood. When you feel that others are unable or unwilling to empathize with you, it may revivify the feeling of being disconnected that first occured in childhood. Like shame, the pain and emotional flooding triggered by feeling a lack of empathy can have deep roots.

A study done in 1978 by Edward Tronick, PhD, director of University of Massachusetts-Boston's Infant-Parent Mental Health Program, and colleagues revealed dramatically the effects of lack of empathy on an infant. Dr. Tronick instructed mothers to withhold responses and keep a "still face" when they were with their infants. When the babies did not get expressive responses from their mothers, they became sad, disengaged, and agitated. This study indicates that people are primed from infancy to need empathy from those close to them and when deprived of it, they can experience emotional flooding. As an adult, you may respond similarly to a lack of empathy from those close to you.

When you are experiencing emotional flooding due to a lack of empathy from someone close to you, we recommend you STOP to use the following tools.

Suggested Tool Set				
LACK OF EMPATHY FROM ANOTHER Audio Track 31	Tool 1 Mindfulness with Detached Observation, p. 83	Tool 5 Imaginary Support Circle, p. 93	Tool 6 Wise Self, p. 95	Tool 12 Self-Statements, p. 108

Generating Self-Statements:
Feeling a Lack of Empathy from Another

Recall a time when you experienced a strong reaction to feeling a lack of empathy from another. Notice your thoughts when you were flooded with those feelings. For example, you might have thought, "If he cared about me, he would care about my pain"; "I really am alone in this relationship"; or "It hurts that she doesn't get it and doesn't care."

Choose a few of those thoughts and write them down on the lines that follow. Feel free to use the earlier examples.

Thought 1:

_____

Thought 2:

_____

Thought 3:

_____

Thought 4:

_____

Thought 5:

_____

Now use the thoughts you've written to generate the self-statements you can use in Tool 12 to de-escalate your emotional flooding. Simply write the opposite of each of your flooding-immersed thoughts. For example, "He shows his caring in other ways"; "We are deeply connected. I just don't feel it now"; "Just because she doesn't show her empathy the way I want her to, doesn't mean she doesn't care about me"; or "Even though showing empathy is not his strong suit, I have other people in my life who can empathize with me, and I can empathize with myself."

Statement 1:

_____

Statement 2:

_____

Statement 3:

_____

Statement 4:

_____

Statement 5:

_____

Next pick the three statements that feel the most powerful, meaningful, or helpful to you. You now have your empathy-related self-statements for Tool 12. It can also be helpful to transfer them to a note that you can keep with you or enter them into this workbook's companion app on your phone so you'll have easy access whenever and wherever you need them.

Reflections

Describe the situation(s) you elicited that led you to feel a lack of empathy from another.

_____
_____
_____

Who in your life especially raises feelings of a lack of empathy? How do you respond to them?

_____
_____
_____

In what specific situations can you imagine using the self-statements in the future?

_____

_____

_____

FEELING RESENTMENT

Resentment can be defined as bitter indignation at having been treated unfairly. Rather than mobilizing you into positive action, resentment typically does not fuel solutions. It feeds on itself. You may find yourself ruminating on and reliving the real or perceived injury.

Resentment differs from anger. Anger, when harnessed adaptively, fuels a drive to take action to rectify a situation. Resentment, on the other hand, only fuels mounting embitterment. The resentment may continue even after you've resolved the negative interaction that led to it. You just can't seem to let it go. Time and time again your thoughts circle back to how you were mistreated, and before you know it you are on the road to emotional flooding again and again.

When you feel overwhelmed by feelings of resentment, we recommend you STOP to use the following tools.

Suggested Tool Set				
RESENTMENT Audio Track 32	Tool 3 Dialing Down Reactivity, p. 88	Tool 1 Mindfulness with Detached Observation, p. 83	Tool 6 Wise Self, p. 95	Tool 12 Self-Statements, p. 108

Generating Self-Statements: Feeling Resentment

Recall a time when you experienced a strong feeling of resentment. Notice your thoughts when you were flooded with those feelings. For example, you might have thought, "That test was so unfair!"; "I don't deserve to be treated like that"; or "I should have gotten that promotion after all the work I put in." Choose a few of those thoughts and write them down on the lines that follow. Feel free to use the earlier examples.

Thought 1:

_____

Thought 2:

_____

Thought 3:

_____

Thought 4:

_____

Thought 5:

_____

You can use the thoughts you've written to generate the self-statements you can use in Tool 12 to de-escalate resentment-related emotional flooding. To do so, simply write the opposite of each of your flooding-immersed thoughts. For example, "Life isn't always fair"; "I do deserve to be treated well, and I am by most people"; and "Even though I'm disappointed I didn't get the promotion, I am proud of the work I did."

Statement 1:

_____

Statement 2:

_____

Statement 3:

_____

Statement 4:

_____

Statement 5:

_____

Now that you have a list of individualized self-statements for resentment and a few commonly used ones, pick the three that feel the most powerful, meaningful, or helpful to you. You now have your resentment-related self-statements for Tool 12. It can also be helpful to transfer them to a note that you can keep with you or enter them into this workbook's companion app on your phone so you'll have easy access whenever and wherever you need them.

Reflections

Describe the situation(s) you elicited that led you to feel resentment.

_____
_____
_____

Who in your life especially raises feelings of resentment? How do you respond to them?

_____
_____
_____

In what specific situations can you imagine using the self-statements in the future?

_____
_____
_____

FEELING DEFEATED OR HOPELESS

Feeling defeated or helpless in a relationship comes about when you think you are out of options for resolving an impasse. In some cases, you may feel that way even when you actually have options that haven't occurred to you yet. Feelings of defeat limit your creative thinking. Thus, you need to remind yourself that there may be alternative strategies that you haven't considered.

Unfortunately, sometimes there are circumstances that you just can't change, especially in relationships. Although you can ask for what you need, convey what you want, and implore others to respond, you ultimately have no control over others' behaviors. For example, despite your best efforts, you might not be able to get your boss to communicate with you in the way you want. Or, despite your many entreaties, your partner consistently puts work ahead of your family. Regardless of the circumstances, when you consistently fail to find a solution to a relationship problem, you can be left with an overwhelming sense of defeat and hopelessness. This can trigger emotional flooding.

When you feel stuck in defeat and hopelessness due to an impasse in a relationship, we recommend you STOP to use the following tools.

Suggested Tool Set				
FEELING DEFEATED/ HOPELESS Audio Track #33	Tool 8 Remembering Successes, p. 99	Tool 9 Positive Future-Focusing, p. 101	Tool 5 Imaginary Support Circle, p. 93	Tool 12 Self-Statements, p. 108

Generating Self-Statements: Feeling Defeated or Hopeless

Remember a time when you experienced a strong feeling of defeat or hopelessness. Notice your thoughts when you were flooded with those feelings. For example, you might have thought, "I give up. He's never going to change"; "I feel powerless in this situation"; or "I've thought of every possible solution and nothing works." Choose a few of your thoughts and write them down on the lines that follow. Feel free to use the earlier examples.

Thought 1:

_____

Thought 2:

_____

Thought 3:

_____

Thought 4:

_____

Thought 5:

_____

Next you can use the thoughts you've written to generate the self-statements you can use in Tool 12 to de-escalate emotional flooding due to feelings of defeat or hopelessness. To do so, simply write the opposite of each of your flooding-immersed thoughts. For example: "I have more options: we haven't tried couples counseling"; "I'm not hopeless. I can ask others for suggestions"; "I can accept what I cannot change."

Statement 1:

_____

Statement 2:

_____

Statement 3:

_____

Statement 4:

_____

Statement 5:

_____

Now that you have a list of individualized self-statements to use when you're feeling defeated and helpless, pick the three that feel the most powerful, meaningful, or helpful to you. You now have your self-statements for Tool 12 related to feelings of defeat or hopelessness. It can also be helpful to transfer them to a note that you can keep with you or enter them into this workbook's companion app on your phone so you'll have easy access whenever and wherever you need them.

Reflections

Describe the situation(s) you elicited that led you to feel defeated or hopeless.

_____

_____

_____

Who in your life especially raises feelings of defeat or hopelessness? How do you respond to them?

_____

_____

_____

In what specific situations can you imagine using the self-statements in the future?

_____

_____

_____

Take-Away Points

— Humans are not solitary creatures. Your relationships with those close to you can bring both great satisfaction and emotional distress.

— When you are emotionally flooded due to challenges in a relationship, the STOP protocol along with the recommended tools can help soften your reactivity and stop the flooding.

— Know your emotional triggers in relationships and keep the audio tracks containing the tool sets (tracks 18–33) handy at all times.

— Your self-talk is powerful. Therefore, it is vital to identify self-defeating statements and counter them with self-affirming statements related to whatever emotions are flooding your system.

— Keep your self-statements for all triggers handy by using The Road to Calm Companion App or carrying them with you on a sheet of paper.

— Make a copy of the following table, take a picture that you store in your smartphone, or download The Road to Calm Companion App to keep this information with you at all times.

Suggested Tools Sets for Managing Emotional Flooding in Relationships				
FEELING ABANDONED Audio Track 25	Tool 1 Mindfulness with Detached Observation, p. 83	Tool 6 Wise Self, p. 95	Tool 7 Empathic Self, p. 97	Tool 12 Self-Statements, p. 108
FEELINGS OF BETRAYAL Audio Track 26	Tool 3 Dialing Down Reactivity, p. 88	Tool 7 Empathic Self, p. 97	Tool 9 Positive Future-Focusing, p. 101	Tool 12 Self-Statements, p. 108
FEELING CONTROLLED Audio Track 27	Tool 1 Mindfulness with Detached Observation, p. 83	Tool 10 Juxta-position of Two Thoughts or Feelings, p. 103	Tool 3 Dialing Down Reactivity, p. 88	Tool 12 Self-Statements, p. 108

FEELING CRITICIZED Audio Track 28	Tool 8 Remembering Successes, p. 99	Tool 2 Okay Signal, p. 85	Tool 7 Empathic Self, p. 97	Tool 12 Self-Statements, p. 108
FEELING JUDGED/ SHAMED Audio Track 29	Tool 1 Mindfulness with Detached Observation, p. 83	Tool 2 Okay Signal, p. 85	Tool 6 Wise Self, p. 95	Tool 12 Self-Statements, p. 108
FEELING MIS-UNDERSTOOD Audio Track 30	Tool 1 Mindfulness with Detached Observation, p. 83	Tool 7 Empathic Self, p. 97	Tool 10 Juxta-position of Two Thoughts or Feel-ings, p. 103	Tool 12 Self-Statements, p. 108
LACK OF EMPATHY FROM ANOTHER Audio Track 31	Tool 1 Mindfulness with Detached Observation, p. 83	Tool 5 Imaginary Support Circle, p. 93	Tool 6 Wise Self, p. 95	Tool 12 Self-Statements, p. 108
RESENTMENT Audio Track 32	Tool 3 Dialing Down Reactivity, p. 88	Tool 1 Mindfulness with Detached Observation, p. 83	Tool 6 Wise Self, p. 95	Tool 12 Self-Statements, p. 108
FEELING DEFEATED/ HOPELESS Audio Track #33	Tool 8 Remembering Successes, p. 99	Tool 9 Positive Future-Focusing, p. 101	Tool 5 Imaginary Support Circle, p. 93	Tool 12 Self-Statements, p. 108

Cementing Your Success

Good habits are worth being fanatical about.

—JOHN IRVING

STUDIES HAVE SHOWN THAT THE WAY TO CREATE ENDURING CHANGE IS TO use a new skill over and over until it becomes habitual. In this chapter, we focus on the reality that practice makes permanent. Only continued application of the skills you've learned ensures lasting change and, ultimately, personal transformation.

THE BAD NEWS AND THE GOOD NEWS

Catching and changing firmly ingrained emotional reactions is not easy. And the path of least resistance is to maintain existing patterns. That's the bad news.

The good news is that, with repetition, just about any chosen response or action can become habitual and your new default reaction.

Practice Makes Permanent: The Neuroscience

Neuroscientists have learned that repeatedly practicing healthy responses can lead to permanent changes in the way you think, act, and react. This is, in part, because your brain has an astonishing capacity to create new neuronal pathways throughout your lifetime. This is like laying down new pathways through a forest. It might require some trailblazing at first, but eventually the dirt trails that are frequently travelled become so well-worn that they develop pathways for your feet to follow. In the same way, your brain responses follow well-worn paths that become your default responses. Know that if the road you're going down keeps leading to emotional flooding, you have the capacity to create new roads. By practicing the tools you have learned in this workbook, you are developing skills to regulate your emotions, and in the process you are paving new neural pathways. It takes sustained effort and repeated practice of emotional regulation to strengthen the new paths that facilitate emotional regulation. In time, this creates a new default response to the triggers that in the past have led to emotional flooding.

DEALING WITH RESISTANCE

So, to change habitual responses and rewire brain pathways, much practice is needed. When you apply the tools repeatedly, you are creating the grooves in a new roadway, treading and re-treading them into a new default response. However, laying the new pathway is one thing; *taking* it is another.

It can be very difficult to make time to develop and sustain new habits, especially when you are busy or not particularly motivated, even though you know that practicing the tools on a daily basis is beneficial to you. For example, you may know that reducing your sugar consumption and getting regular exercise are good for maintaining a healthy weight. But how often do people slip off the wagon? You already know that implementing a new constructive habit and eliminating the destructive ones can be a challenge. To address this, the following exercises can help make your practice of the Daily Stress Inoculation and the STOP Solution a habit.

RECOMMENDED TOOLS TO MAKE PRACTICE PERMANENT

— Wise Self to Support Practice (adapted from Tool 6)
— Positive Future-Focusing to Support Practice (adapted from Tool 9)
— Self-Statements to Support Practice (adapted from Tool 12)

WISE SELF TO SUPPORT PRACTICE (TOOL 6)

PURPOSE

— Acknowledge that you are capable of accessing a part of yourself that is firm and disciplined.

— Manage any resistance to practice by accessing the wise self to ensure that you keep your commitment to your daily practice and to take time-outs whenever needed.

With Tool 6 you learned to call forth a *wise self*—the part of yourself that is competent, grounded, mature, compassionate, and wise. Accessing this wise part of yourself can come in handy not only when you're flooded, but when you need to access a part of yourself that can be well disciplined. The following exercise will teach you how to call upon the wise self whenever you are in need of an advocate to keep you on track, practicing all the tools that will serve to calm your emotional flooding.

DIRECTIONS

1. Recall in detail a specific instance in which you felt wise and self-disciplined.
2. Bring awareness and attention to what it felt like when you engaged this disciplined part of yourself.
3. Recognize that you can access this mature part of yourself whenever you need to help inform your actions and help to keep yourself on track practicing the tools.
4. Engage this part of yourself, bringing attention and awareness to what it feels like when this part of yourself is present and active.

Listen to the recording for audio track 34.

Reflections

What specific instance of self-discipline did you recall? Where were you? What were you struggling with doing? What was the context of the situation? Be as detailed as possible.

_____

_____

_____

What is it like for you to access that disciplined, kind, but firm part of yourself?

_____

_____

_____

In what specific circumstances in the future do you anticipate using the Wise Self? Be as detailed as possible.

_____

_____

_____

POSITIVE FUTURE-FOCUSING TO SUPPORT PRACTICE (TOOL 9)

PURPOSE

— Harness the intention to interrupt emotional flooding as soon as it occurs

— Associate satisfaction and pride with engaging in a consistent practice of the tools

— Maintain the habit of using the tools on a regular basis

It is crucial to create an intention that will help you consistently implement the tools to manage your emotional flooding. You have already learned to use the skill of positive future-focusing, fast-forwarding in your mind's eye to a time in the future when your emotional flooding has dissipated. With the following exercise, you can harness this skill to serve you in a different way, fast-forwarding to a time in the near future when you are engaging the tools successfully: practicing the daily stress inoculation; initiating time-outs; noticing yourself enacting the tools with ease and skill; and reaping the benefits of all your work as the power of each of the tools to eliminate emotional flooding increases with repeated use.

DIRECTIONS

1. Experience in this moment the satisfaction of adhering to a desired habit.
2. Imagine a positive future when the benefits of your practice enable you to quickly regain emotional equilibrium.

Listen to the recording for audio track 35.

Reflections

What was your experience when you fast-forwarded to a time in the future when you were actively using the tools to manage your emotional flooding? What feelings emerged when you envisioned this time in the future as if it were happening now?

_____

_____

_____

In what specific circumstances in the future might this tool be especially helpful (i.e., when you're particularly unmotivated due to being tired, stressed, busy, etc.)?

_____

_____

_____

SELF-STATEMENTS TO SUPPORT PRACTICE (TOOL 12)

PURPOSE

— Harness the power of your words.

— Recognize and reaffirm that you are capable of generating positive statements that help you consistently use the tools.

— Face and overcome any resistance to the consistent implementation of the tools.

By now, you've created self-statements for a number of triggers that send you into emotional overwhelm and have used these self-statements to close your time-outs. Self-statements solidify your success in quelling your emotional flooding at the end of each time-out. They also prepare you to reengage with the world and continue with your day from an emotionally regulated standpoint.

Self-statements also are essential to bolster your motivation to _initiate_ time-outs (and the Daily Stress Inoculation) on a consistent basis in your daily life. Whenever you're feeling stuck in resistance, self-statements offer a quick and effective way to get back on track. You can play the self-statements (audio track 36) or simply repeat the needed statements independent of the audio whenever the need arises.

Emile Coué, the renowned French pharmacist who practiced hypnosis in the early twentieth century, asserted that any idea exclusively occupying the mind turns into reality.

Generating Self-Statements: Supporting Practice

Elicit a memory of a time when you just couldn't force yourself to take some action that you knew you needed to do for your best interest. Recall the thoughts that accompanied this memory of inaction or procrastination. For example, you might have thought, "I just can't get myself to do this," "I'm too busy to do this now," or "I know I should, but I'd rather watch TV."

Choose a few of your thoughts and write them down on the lines that follow. Feel free to use the earlier examples.

Thought 1:

_____

Thought 2:

_____

Thought 3:

_____

Thought 4:

_____

Thought 5:

_____

Now, use the thoughts you've written to generate the self-statements for Tool 12 to enhance your commitment to implement the tools in your daily life. To do so, write a compassionate, encouraging statement in response to each of your statements related to resistance or procrastination. For example, "I take time to honor my need to take care of myself"; "I look forward to experiencing relaxation, calm and receptivity to new perspectives"; and "I am using the tools because it's important to me that emotional flooding no longer controls me." Feel free to use the examples given.

Statement 1:

_____

Statement 2:

_____

Statement 3:

_____

Statement 4:

_____

Statement 5:

_____

Now that you have a list of individualized self-statements, choose the three that feel the most powerful, meaningful, or helpful to you. You now have your self-statements to reinforce your practice for Tool 12.

Listen to the recording for audio track 36.

What was your experience using the self-statements your created to overcome any resistance to practicing the tools?

_____

_____

_____

How does your negative running commentary affect the choices you make in your actions or habits? How do your positive self-statements help you keep your commitments to yourself?

_____

_____

_____

Yes, You Can Teach an Old Dog New Tricks

"We become what we repeatedly do."   —SEAN COVEY

Practice, lots and lots of repeated practice, is the key to effectively retraining your brain and your emotional responses. However, you need to be willing and committed to notice and interrupt any runaway emotions quickly and then to practice new and healthy responses. Yes, you *can* interrupt your default patterns, which are easily triggered and result in emotional overwhelm. Yes, you can *permanently* establish new responses in your emotional repertoire. So practice makes permanent. This is how lasting change comes to fruition and is maintained.

Permanent—Not Perfect

"Respect your efforts, respect yourself. Self-respect leads to self-discipline.
When you have both firmly under your belt, that's real power."   —CLINT EASTWOOD

You may be familiar with the phrase *practice makes perfect*. Perfection, however, is not generally in the repertoire of human beings. You are not merely rational. Rather, your actions and interactions are fueled by a wonderful mix of logic and emotion. This is why you, like everyone, make mistakes. You step on the toes of others. You make choices that logically aren't always in your best interests, and you have the capacity to feel emotion intensely. This is all part of being human. Healthy interaction, then, isn't about never making a mistake. It's about your ability to maintain a balance between the intensity of your emotional response and the degree of threat present; your ability to fall in and out of connection in relationship, making mistakes and then reconnecting, reattuning, and returning to emotional equilibrium.

The goal of emotional regulation is not to become void of emotion. Rather, it is to moderate the intensity of your reactions to the inevitable triggers in your life, so that you can experience your emotions fully, without fear that they will engulf you. As you teach yourself to patiently and consistently handle your emotions without excessive reactivity, you cultivate a secure and grounded internal environment that can transform your life.

Take-Away Points

- Practice, lots and lots of repeated practice, is the key to effectively retrain your brain and change your emotional responses.
- *Knowing* that something is in your best interest and *doing* it are two different things.
- Use the adaptations of Tools 6, 9, and 12 to enhance your motivation to practice the DSI and the STOP Solution.

Resources

ONLINE RESOURCES

The Web sites of the following associations, organizations, and foundations provide a plethora of resources and self-help suggestions.

Anxiety and Depression Association of America
www.adaa.org

Anxieties.com
www.anxieties.com

Benson-Henry Institute for Mind Body Medicine
www.mgh.harvard.edu/bhi

Depression and Bipolar Support Alliance
www.dbsalliance.org

International OCD Foundation
www.ocfoundation.org

International Society for the Study of Traumatic Stress and Dissociation
www.isst-d.org

Mindfulness Associates
www.mindfulnessassociates.com

National Alliance on Mental Illness
www.nami.org

National Anger Management Association
www.namass.org

National Center for PTSD

www.ptsd.va.gov

Social Phobia/Social Anxiety Association

www.socialphobia.org

BOOKS

ANGER

Carter, L., & Minirth, E. (2012). *The anger workbook*. Nashville, TN: Thomas Nelson.

McKay, M., & Rogers, P. (2000). *The anger control workbook*. Oakland, CA: New Harbinger.

ANXIETY

Antony, M., Craske, M., & Barlow, D. (2006). *Mastering your fears and phobias: Workbook (Treatments that work)* (2nd ed.). New York, NY: Oxford University Press.

Antony, M., & Norton, P. (2009). *The anti-anxiety workbook: Proven strategies to overcome worry, phobias, panic, and obsession*. New York, NY: Guilford Press.

Bourne, E. (1995). *The anxiety & phobia workbook*. Oakland, CA: New Harbinger.

Burns, D. (2006). *When panic attacks: The new, drug-free anxiety therapy that can change your life*. Morgan Road Books.

Daitch, C. (2011). *Anxiety disorders: The go-to guide for clients and therapists*. New York, NY: Norton.

Davis, M., Eshelman, E., & McKay, M. (1982). *The relaxation and stress reduction workbook*. Oakland, CA: New Harbinger.

Foa, E., & Wilson, R. (2001). *Stop obsessing! How to overcome your obsessions and compulsions*. New York, NY: Bantam Books.

Forsyth, J., & Eifert, G. (2007). *The mindfulness and acceptance workbook for anxiety*. Oakland, CA: New Harbinger.

Heyman, B., & Pedrick, C. (1999). *The OCD workbook: Your guide to breaking free from obsessive-compulsive disorders*. Oakland, CA: New Harbinger.

Weeks, C. (1990). *Hope and help for your nerves*. New York, NY: Signet.

Wehrenberg, M. (2012). *The 10 best-ever anxiety management techniques workbook*. New York, NY: Norton.

Wilson, R. (1996). *Don't panic: Taking control of anxiety attacks* (rev. ed.). New York, NY: Harper/Perennial Library.

BRAIN AND NEUROSCIENCE

Goleman, D. (2003). *Destructive emotions*. New York, NY: Bantam Books.

LeDoux, J. (1996). *The emotional brain: The mysterious underpinnings of emotional life*. New York, NY: Simon & Schuster.

Nhat Hanh, T. (1975). *The miracle of mindfulness*. Boston, MA: Beacon.

Siegel, D. (2007). *The mindful brain: Reflection and attunement in the cultivation of well-being*. New York, NY: Norton.

DEPRESSION

Burns, D. D. (2008). *Feeling good: The new mood therapy*. New York, NY: HarperCollins.

Copeland, M. E., & MacKay, M. (2002). *The depression workbook: A guide for living with depression and manic depression* (2nd ed.). Oakland, CA: New Harbinger.

Williams, M., Teasdale, J., Zindel, S., & Kabat-Zinn, J. (2007). *The mindful way through depression: Freeing yourself from chronic unhappiness*. New York, NY: Guilford Press.

Zetin, M., Hoepner, T., & Kurth, J. (2010). *Challenging depression: The go-to guide for clinicians and patients*. New York, NY: Norton.

ENHANCING RELATIONSHIPS

Daitch, C., & Lorberbaum, L. (2012). *Anxious in love: How to manage your anxiety, reduce conflict, and reconnect with your partner*. Oakland, CA: New Harbinger.

Fruzzetti, A., & Linehan, M. (2006). *The high-conflict couple: A dialectical behavior therapy guide to finding peace, intimacy, & validation*. Oakland, CA: New Harbinger.

Gottman, J. (1994). *Why marriages succeed or fail*. New York, NY: Simon & Schuster.

Gottman, J., & Silver, N. (1999). *The seven principles for making marriage work*. New York, NY: Three Rivers Press.

Hendrix, H. (2007). *Getting the love you want: A guide for couples, 20th anniversary edition*. New York, NY: Henry Holt.

Hunt, H., & Hendrix, H. (2003). *Getting the love you want workbook*. New York, NY: Atria Books.

Siegel, D. (2012). *Pocket guide to interpersonal neurobiology: An integrative handbook of the mind*. New York, NY: W. W. Norton.

Siegel, D. (2012). *The developing mind: How relationships and the brain interact to shape who we are* (2nd ed.). New York, NY: Guilford Press.

Zeig, J., & Kulbatski, T. (2011). *Ten commandments for couples: For every aspect of your relationship journey*. Phoenix, AZ: Zeig, Tucker & Theisen.

MANAGING EMOTIONS

Benson, H. (1984). *Beyond the relaxation response*. New York, NY: Times Books.

Daitch, C. (2007). *Affect regulation toolbox: Practical and effective hypnotic interventions for the over-reactive client*. New York, NY: W.W. Norton.

Kabat-Zinn, J. (1991). *Full catastrophe living: Using the wisdom of your body and mind to face stress, pain and illness*. McHenry, IL: Delta.

Teasdale, J., Williams, M., & Segal, Z. (2014). *The mindful way workbook: An 8-week program to free yourself from depression and emotional distress*. New York, NY: Guilford Press.

AUDIO RECORDINGS

Many of the tools and procedures described in this book are available in the CD programs listed here. To order these audio programs, contact:

The Center for the Treatment of Anxiety Disorders

E-mail: canxietydisorders@me.com

www.carolyndaitchphd.com or www.anxiety-treatment.com

or search iTunes

Daitch, C. (Speaker) (2009). *Alpha/Theta Sailing II* [CD]. Farmington Hills, MI: Center for the Treatment of Anxiety Disorders.

This CD is especially useful for clients and clinicians who are using guided imagery, progressive relaxation, or hypnosis. It is designed to assist the client to quickly move into a state conducive to the development of therapist- or self-directed experience. With repeated exposure in therapy sessions, the music becomes a cue for the client to elicit a state of relaxation.

Daitch, C. (Speaker) (2003). *Dialing Down Anxiety* [CD]. Farmington Hills, MI: Center for the Treatment of Anxiety Disorders.

This audio program utilizes visualization, guided imagery, and established stress and anxiety reduction techniques to counter the over-reactivity that accompanies anxiety.

Daitch, C. (Speaker) (2013). *Test Anxiety Solutions* [CD]. Farmington Hills, MI: Center for the Treatment of Anxiety Disorders and Catherine Herzog.

This recording is designed to help the listener master excessive anxiety over taking exams. You will learn to relax your nervous system while remaining alert and focused when you prepare for and take exams.

Daitch, C. (Speaker) (2013). *Overcoming Emotional Eating: Breaking the cycle of stress and anxiety based eating* [CD]. Farmington Hills, MI: Mindfulness Associates and Catherine Herzog.

This audio program teaches the listener to discriminate emotionally based cravings from real hunger. The program provides a set of tools to help the listener manage the stress, anxiety, and other emotions that lead to overeating.

Daitch, C. (Speaker) (2003). *The Insomnia Solution* [CD]. Farmington Hills, MI: Mindfulness Associates.

This audio program guides the listener into a relaxed state and the requisite stillness of mind and body necessary for sleep. When used nightly, the listener can train his or her nervous system to elicit the appropriate level of relaxation to foster good sleep habits.

Naparstek, B. (1995). *Meditations to Relieve Stress.* Health Journeys.

This recording uses four exercises to help master anxiety and promote feelings of safety and protection. www.healthjourneys.com

Naparstek, B. (2007). *Guided Meditations for Help with Panic Attacks.* Health Journeys.

> *This audio program uses healing imagery to reduce or eliminate acute anxiety and panic attacks. www.healthjourneys.com*

Yapko, M. *Calm Down: A Self-Help Program for Managing Anxiety.* Michael D. Yapko, PhD.

> *This audio program includes four CDs that teach self-hypnosis for reducing anxiety. www.yapko.com*

REFERRALS TO THERAPISTS

The following organizations have a list of therapists and contact information.

The American Society of Clinical Hypnosis (ASCH)
www.asch.net

Association for Behavioral and Cognitive Therapies (ABCT)
www.abct.org

Association for Contextual Behavioral Science
www.contextualpsychology.org/act

National Association of Cognitive Behavioral Therapy (NACBT)
www.nacbt.org

Relational Somatic Psychotherapy
www.threefoldway.com

The Society of Clinical and Experimental Hypnosis (SCEH)
www. sceh.us

UCLA Mindful Awareness Research Center
www.marc.ucla.edu/

United States Association of Body Psychotherapy
www.usabp.org

Table of Tool Sets

Suggested Tool Sets for Managing Emotional Stressors			
WORRY Audio Track 18	Tool 1 Mindfulness with Detached Observation, p. 83	Tool 3 Dialing Down Reactivity, p. 88	Tool 11 Postponement, p. 105	Tool 12 Self-Statements, p. 108
PANIC Audio Track 19	Tool 1 Mindfulness with Detached Observation, p. 83	Tool 4 Heavy Hands, Heavy Legs, p. 91	Tool 9 Positive Future-Focusing, p. 101	Tool 12 Self-Statements, p. 108
INTOLERANCE OF BODILY DISTRESS Audio Track 20	Tool 1 Mindfulness with Detached Observation, p. 83	Tool 2 Okay Signal, p. 85	Tool 4 Heavy Hands, Heavy Legs, p. 91	Tool 12 Self-Statements, p. 108
LONELINESS Audio Track 21	Tool 5 Imaginary Support Circle, p. 93	Tool 6 Wise Self, p. 95	Tool 10 Juxta-position of Two Thoughts or Feel-ings, p. 103	Tool 12 Self-Statements, p. 108
HOPELESSNESS Audio Track 22	Tool 8 Remembering Successes, p. 99	Tool 6 Wise Self, p. 95	Tool 9 Positive Future-Focusing, p. 101	Tool 12 Self-Statements, p. 108
FRUSTRATION Audio Track 23	Tool 3 Dialing Down Reactivity, p. 88	Tool 2 Okay Signal, p. 85	Tool 6 Wise Self, p. 95	Tool 12 Self-Statements, p. 108
EXPLOSIVE ANGER Audio Track 24	Tool 4 Heavy Hands, Heavy Legs, p. 91	Tool 3 Dialing Down Reactivity, p. 88	Tool 6 Wise Self, p. 95	Tool 12 Self-Statements, p. 108

Suggested Tools Sets for Managing Emotional Flooding in Relationships				
FEELING ABANDONED Audio Track 25	Tool 1 Mindfulness with Detached Observation, p. 83	Tool 6 Wise Self, p. 95	Tool 7 Empathic Self, p. 97	Tool 12 Self-Statements, p. 108
FEELINGS OF BETRAYAL Audio Track 26	Tool 3 Dialing Down Reactivity, p. 88	Tool 7 Empathic Self, p. 97	Tool 9 Positive Future-Focusing, p. 101	Tool 12 Self-Statements, p. 108
FEELING CONTROLLED Audio Track 27	Tool 1 Mindfulness with Detached Observation, p. 83	Tool 10 Juxta-position of Two Thoughts or Feel-ings, p. 101	Tool 3 Dialing Down Reactivity, p. 88	Tool 12 Self-Statements, p. 108
FEELING CRITICIZED Audio Track 28	Tool 8 Remembering Successes, p. 99	Tool 2 Okay Signal, p. 85	Tool 7 Empathic Self, p. 97	Tool 12 Self-Statements, p. 108
FEELING JUDGED/ SHAMED Audio Track 29	Tool 1 Mindfulness with Detached Observation, p. 83	Tool 2 Okay Signal, p. 85	Tool 6 Wise Self, p. 95	Tool 12 Self-Statements, p. 108
FEELING MIS-UNDERSTOOD Audio Track 30	Tool 1 Mindfulness with Detached Observation, p. 83	Tool 7 Empathic Self, p. 97	Tool 10 Juxta-position of Two Thoughts or Feel-ings, p. 103	Tool 12 Self-Statements, p. 108
LACK OF EMPATHY FROM ANOTHER Audio Track 31	Tool 1 Mindfulness with Detached Observation, p. 83	Tool 5 Imaginary Support Circle, p. 93	Tool 6 Wise Self, p. 95	Tool 12 Self-Statements, p. 108

RESENTMENT Audio Track 32	Tool 3 Dialing Down Reactivity, p. 88	Tool 1 Mindfulness with Detached Observation, p. 83	Tool 6 Wise Self, p. 95	Tool 12 Self-Statements, p. 108
FEELING DEFEATED/ HOPELESS Audio Track #33	Tool 8 Remembering Successes, p. 99	Tool 9 Positive Future-Focusing, p. 101	Tool 5 Imaginary Support Circle, p. 93	Tool 12 Self-Statements, p. 108

Identifying Triggers in Relationships: Additional Blank Inventory Sheets

If you ran out of room in the space provided for your relationship inventories at the end of Chapter 3, you can use the following.

In the following inventories, circle the appropriate number for each emotion possibly causing flooding.

In my relationship with _____.

I felt	Never	Rarely	Sometimes	Frequently	Almost Always
abandoned	1	2	3	4	5
betrayed	1	2	3	4	5
controlled	1	2	3	4	5
criticized	1	2	3	4	5
lack of empathy	1	2	3	4	5
judged/shamed	1	2	3	4	5
betrayed	1	2	3	4	5
misunderstood	1	2	3	4	5
resentful	1	2	3	4	5
defeated/hopeless	1	2	3	4	5

For any trigger for which you circled a 4 or 5, fill in the following tables. If there were more than three such triggers, continue writing on a separate sheet of paper. In addition, if there is a trigger that does not occur often but is highly painful when it does occur, add it to the following table.

Trigger	Painful Thoughts and Feelings That Come Up in Response

Often following painful thoughts and feelings in response to a trigger, you might react by becoming defensive or withdrawing (see List of Defensive/Withdrawing Behaviors in Chapter 3).

For the same triggers you entered in the chart, describe your defensive or withdrawing behavior.

Trigger	Ways in Which I Become Defensive and/or Withdraw

In my relationship with _____.

I felt	Never	Rarely	Sometimes	Frequently	Almost Always
abandoned	1	2	3	4	5
betrayed	1	2	3	4	5
controlled	1	2	3	4	5
criticized	1	2	3	4	5
lack of empathy	1	2	3	4	5

judged/shamed	1	2	3	4	5
betrayed	1	2	3	4	5
misunderstood	1	2	3	4	5
resentful	1	2	3	4	5
defeated/hopeless	1	2	3	4	5

For any trigger for which you circled a 4 or 5, fill in the following tables. If there were more than three such triggers, continue writing on a separate sheet of paper. In addition, if there is a trigger that does not occur often but is highly painful when it does occur, add it to the following table.

Trigger	Painful Thoughts and Feelings That Come Up in Response

Often following painful thoughts and feelings in response to a trigger, you might react by becoming defensive or withdrawing (see List of Defensive/Withdrawing Behaviors in Chapter 3).

For the same triggers you entered in the chart, describe your defensive or withdrawing behavior.

Trigger	Ways in Which I Become Defensive and/or Withdraw

In my relationship with _____.

I felt	Never	Rarely	Sometimes	Frequently	Almost Always
abandoned	1	2	3	4	5
betrayed	1	2	3	4	5
controlled	1	2	3	4	5
criticized	1	2	3	4	5
lack of empathy	1	2	3	4	5
judged/shamed	1	2	3	4	5
betrayed	1	2	3	4	5
misunderstood	1	2	3	4	5
resentful·	1	2	3	4	5
defeated/hopeless	1	2	3	4	5

For any trigger for which you circled a 4 or 5, fill in the following tables. If there were more than three such triggers, continue writing on a separate sheet of paper. In addition, if there is a trigger that does not occur often but is highly painful when it does occur, add it to the following table.

Trigger	Painful Thoughts and Feelings That Come Up in Response

Often following painful thoughts and feelings in response to a trigger, you might react by becoming defensive or withdrawing (see List of Defensive/Withdrawing Behaviors in Chapter 3).

For the same triggers you entered in the chart, describe your defensive or withdrawing behavior.

Trigger	Ways in Which I Become Defensive and/or Withdraw

In my relationship with _____.

I felt	Never	Rarely	Sometimes	Frequently	Almost Always
abandoned	1	2	3	4	5
betrayed	1	2	3	4	5
controlled	1	2	3	4	5
criticized	1	2	3	4	5
lack of empathy	1	2	3	4	5
judged/shamed	1	2	3	4	5
betrayed	1	2	3	4	5
misunderstood	1	2	3	4	5
resentful	1	2	3	4	5
defeated/hopeless	1	2	3	4	5

For any trigger for which you circled a 4 or 5, fill in the following tables. If there were more than three such triggers, continue writing on a separate sheet of paper. In addition, if there is a trigger that does not occur often but is highly painful when it does occur, add it to the table.

Trigger	Painful Thoughts and Feelings That Come Up in Response

Often following painful thoughts and feelings in response to a trigger, you might react by becoming defensive or withdrawing (see List of Defensive/Withdrawing Behaviors in Chapter 3).

For the same triggers you entered in the chart, describe your defensive or withdrawing behavior.

Trigger	Ways in Which I Become Defensive and/or Withdraw

In my relationship with _____.

I felt	Never	Rarely	Sometimes	Frequently	Almost Always
abandoned	1	2	3	4	5
betrayed	1	2	3	4	5
controlled	1	2	3	4	5
criticized	1	2	3	4	5
lack of empathy	1	2	3	4	5

judged/shamed	1	2	3	4	5
betrayed	1	2	3	4	5
misunderstood	1	2	3	4	5
resentful	1	2	3	4	5
defeated/hopeless	1	2	3	4	5

For any trigger for which you circled a 4 or 5, fill in the following tables. If there were more than three such triggers, continue writing on a separate sheet of paper. In addition, if there is a trigger that does not occur often but is highly painful when it does occur, add it to the table.

Trigger	Painful Thoughts and Feelings That Come Up in Response

Often following painful thoughts and feelings in response to a trigger, you might react by becoming defensive or withdrawing (see List of Defensive/Withdrawing Behaviors in Chapter 3).

For the same triggers you entered in the chart, describe your defensive or withdrawing behavior.

Trigger	Ways in Which I Become Defensive and/or Withdraw

In my relationship with _____.

I felt	Never	Rarely	Sometimes	Frequently	Almost Always
abandoned	1	2	3	4	5
betrayed	1	2	3	4	5
controlled	1	2	3	4	5
criticized	1	2	3	4	5
lack of empathy	1	2	3	4	5
judged/shamed	1	2	3	4	5
betrayed	1	2	3	4	5
misunderstood	1	2	3	4	5
resentful	1	2	3	4	5
defeated/hopeless	1	2	3	4	5

For any trigger for which you circled a 4 or 5, fill in the following tables. If there were more than three such triggers, continue writing on a separate sheet of paper. In addition, if there is a trigger that does not occur often but is highly painful when it does occur, add it to the table.

Trigger	Painful Thoughts and Feelings That Come Up in Response

Often following painful thoughts and feelings in response to a trigger, you might
Often following painful thoughts and feelings in response to a trigger, you might react by becoming defensive or withdrawing (see List of Defensive/ Withdrawing Behaviors in Chapter 3).

For the same triggers you entered in the chart, describe your defensive or withdrawing behavior.

Trigger	Ways in Which I Become Defensive and/or Withdraw

References

Coué, E. (1922). *The Coué "method": Self-mastery through conscious autosuggestion, complete and unabridged* (A. Stark van Orden, trans.). New York: Malkan Publishing.

Daitch, C., & Lorberbaum, L. (2012). *Anxious in love: How to manage your anxiety, reduce conflict, and reconnect with your partner.* Oakland, CA: New Harbinger.

Hendrix, H. (2010). *Stay in the boat and paddle: Advice for couples from Harville Hendrix, Ph.D.* Retrieved June 2015, from http://www.harvillehendrix. com/read.html

LeDoux, J. (1996). *The emotional brain: The mysterious underpinnings of emotional life.* New York, NY: Simon & Schuster.

Perry, B., & Szalavitz, M. (2006). *The boy who was raised as a dog: And other stories from a child psychiatrist's notebook.* New York, NY: Basic Books.

Schore, A. N. (1996). The experience-dependent maturation of a regulatory system in the orbital prefrontal cortex and the origin of developmental psychopathology. *Development and Psychopathology, 8*, 59–87.

Siegel, D. (2007). *The mindful brain: Reflection and attunement in the cultivation of well-being.* New York, NY: Norton.

Spiegel, H. (1972). An eye-roll test for hypnotizability. *American Journal of Clinical Hypnosis, 15*(1), 25–28.

Tronick, E., Als, H., Adamson, L., Wise, S., & Brazelton, T. B. (1978). Infants' response to entrapment between contradictory messages in face-to-face interaction. *Journal of the American Academy of Child and Adolescent Psychiatry, 17*, 1–13.

Index

Note: Italicized page locators refer to figures.